Outside the Lines

Outside the Lines

How Embracing Queerness Will
Transform Your Faith

Mihee Kim-Kort

Fortress Press
Minneapolis

OUTSIDE THE LINES
How Embracing Queerness Will Transform Your Faith

Cover design: Paul Soupiset

Print ISBN: 978-1-5064-0896-5
eBook ISBN: 978-1-5064-0897-2

The paper used in this publication meets the minimum requirements of American National Standard for Information Sciences — Permanence of Paper for Printed Library Materials, ANSI Z329.48-1984.

Manufactured in the U.S.A.

To Andy

Contents

Acknowledgments

I started this book around the winter of 2015, not really knowing where it would take me. Here it is nearly 2018, three years later, and I'm full of wonder and gratitude. The old adage about how "it takes a village to raise a child" is definitely true in this case, for me, for this book. So many people were my muses and angels; they held my feet to the fire and cheered me on, especially toward the end. While there are too many to name here, I want to thank these beloved ones in particular:

My sisters who form a hedge of protection around me, my tribe and community, who have walked hand-in-hand, heart-to-heart with me these last few years: Jodi Houge, Kerlin Richter, Emily Scott, Austin Channing Brown, Jes Kast, Nadia Bolz-Weber, Nichole Flores, Rachel Kurtz, Neichelle Guidry, Tiffany Thomas, Rozella White, Winnie Varghese, Rachel Held Evans.

Friends with connections to Bloomington who hold it down for me, who know me inside and out, and who teach me more and more about friendship, dedication, and life together: Christie Popp, April Hennessey, Rachel Varon, Tanya Kennedy, Meg Foster, Tiffany Roman, Ashley Miller.

Friends and loved ones near and far who get me so deeply and push me to not hold back: Jeff Chu, Kenji Kuramitsu, Erica Liu, Larissa Kwong Abazia, Katie Baker, Joanna Kim, Laura Cheifetz, Chris Hong, Grace Ji-Sun Kim.

The team at Fortress Press, especially my patient and dedicated editor, Lisa Kloskin, who combed through my words providing honest and critical feedback, and most importantly, talked me off the ledge numerous times when I felt ready to abandon the whole project. I could not have done this without them.

My family, whom I love and adore always: my parents, Yong and Son, who spent countless hours with the children so I could make some semblance of sense with this jumble of words; my brother, Joseph; my sister-in-law, Nayoung; and my in-laws, Tom, Corrine, and Sarah.

Last but certainly never least, my spouse, Andy, for walking with me through so many questions and being faithfully and intimately present in it all, and my children, Desmond, Anna, and Oswald, for all the ways you show me that love keeps coming.

Foreword

The word *hospitable* may seem more suited for describing a cozy coffee shop or comfortable guest room than a person, but as I've traveled the world and met many of its inhabitants, I've found that there are just some people with whom you always feel at home. Mihee Kim-Kort is one of those people. Warm, thoughtful, curious, and brave, Mihee immediately sets those around her at ease. To be in her presence is to be in the presence of a friend, whether you've known her your whole life, for just ten minutes, or like me, through many years of correspondence and collaboration. A typical conversation with Mihee is likely to meander comfortably from the challenges of ministry to the daily adventures of parenthood, to the real-life implications of incarnational theology and gender theory. At some point, you will probably end up spilling your guts, because with Mihee, you know your most sacred and tender stories are safe. That's no small thing.

It was a true delight to recognize so much of the woman I know in "real life" in the pages of the book you now hold in your hands. *Outside the Lines* is a beautifully crafted work of hospitality that manages to be at once provocative and comforting, a challenge and a relief. With disarming vulnerability, Mihee weaves together stories from her own life with profound insights from Christian theology, biblical studies, and queer spirituality, to lead the reader into a richer understanding of this complex, mysterious, and indeed *queer* world God has created. It's rare to find a book on gender and sexuality that is this intellectually rigorous and this relatable. There were passages that made me pause to think, passages that made me laugh, passages that took my breath away. I finished certain I was better prepared to love God, my neighbor, and myself.

For many, this book will be an eye-opener. For others, especially those whose identities and self-understanding fall "outside the lines," it will be a lifesaver. It is, ultimately, a book about love—the "real and actual, in-the-flesh-and-blood-and-tears love," as Mihee puts it, that we experience in our relationships with one another and with Jesus, who breaks every boundary to welcome us into his body.

I find it fitting that the word *hospitable* shares its roots with the word *hospital*, for the most welcoming people in our lives are always ultimately healers. With this book, Mihee offers both an antidote and a balm—an antidote to the poisonous lies that the culture and the church tell us about our bodies and our identities, and a balm to soothe and heal the pain those lies have caused. What a gift this work is to the church and to the world.

So, even if you're a little intimidated by the path ahead, reader, read on! You are in the most capable and loving hands.

Rachel Held Evans

Introduction

Why queer?

More than a decade ago, I went with a good friend to visit a photographer she was checking out for her wedding. I was dressed in my usual T-shirt, shorts, and sandals, with my long hair loose and no makeup. As my friend and the photographer discussed the calendar, I was standing in the waiting room with my back turned to them, looking at the photographs on the wall. At one point, I heard the photographer say to my friend, "Do you want to ask your fiancé if *he* wants to come and look at these samples?" I turned around and looked at her quizzically. When she realized she had made a mistake, she turned bright red with embarrassment and apologized profusely to both of us.

Though I laughed awkwardly, I was devastated and ashamed, because this misunderstanding wasn't new to me. I have often felt a disconnect between the internal and external—emotionally, physically, even spiritually—between my internal experience of myself and the way others perceived me as I interacted and connected with them. For a long while, I had experienced the incongruity that what I felt on the inside didn't always match what people read, saw, interpreted, or understood on the surface of my life.

These days, for the most part, to the world I read cisgender (identifying with the gender that was assigned at birth) and heterosexual. I intentionally fulfilled those scripts in adulthood by getting an education, getting a job, getting married (to a man), having kids, and getting a house. I grew up in the most traditional and conventional Korean immigrant family—Christian, hardworking, morally upstanding, and hardly making any waves. On the surface, I appear to be very clear on my identity, my ministry and work, my faith, and my passions and desires. So why does queerness matter to me?

I have to confess the privileges I have because of my status. I've never experienced discrimination, harassment, or violence because of my sexual identity in the way many LGBTQIA people—especially LGBTQIA people of color —have suffered abuse, violence, oppression, prejudice, and persecution. The number of deaths of transgender women of color around the world is increasing every day. As I write this, LGBTQIA youth make up a large percentage of the homeless population across the country, and that statistic increases every day. Queerness matters because it is a matter of life and death.

Growing up, I never made the word *queer* a part of my vocabulary. It felt like a word that belonged in Shakespearean times, a word that my friends' grandmothers would use to describe anything strange and peculiar. In high school, I would hear it used interchangeably with *gay*. People would say, "That's gay!" or, "Don't be so queer!" to express discomfort and judgment of anything that was strange—especially something that deviated from norms around gender and sexual identity. When said out loud, the word was colored with streaks of contempt. It sounded like a curse word. To be queer was to be undesirable.

Yet, like so much that is dismissed or rejected, queerness found a way to take root and grow. The people who first started talking about queerness didn't do so in ivory towers. Concepts of queerness came out of flesh-and-blood lives, from broken hearts and crushed spirits, from the ordinary material of everyday life. So it is the streets and neighborhoods, workplaces and schools, parks and playgrounds, courthouses and churches that I'm concerned with in this project. It is where people reside and, in those spaces, how people interact and comprehend one another, reading bodies, lives, and stories.

Of course, concepts of queerness have been explored by scholars, and I am deeply indebted to their work, especially *After Sex: On Writing since Queer Theory*.[1] As with any theoretical framework, there are limitations to how we can define queerness, and the concept is shifting all the time. Queerness has undergone numerous challenges and transformations. It began as a way to describe certain expressions of sexuality and gender, and now it includes other markers of identity, such as race, ethnicity, nationality, ability, and more. Yes, it's rooted in matters of gender and sexuality, but queerness is not meant to be exclusionary. In fact, any kind of exclusion would be counter to queerness, because queerness is about bodies, and we all have bodies. We move through this world in our bodies, and we're constantly interacting with other bodies. This matters.

To me, queerness is three things:

It is a *posture*. Queerness transgresses boundaries and allows us to simply be, without label or category, specifically around gender and sexuality. Queer is at odds with the normal, the legitimate, the dominant. It is particular and expansive. It's less definitive; it does not point to you or me and say, "You are queer," but instead makes a wide-open space for all people to find footing in relation to one another and their own lives.

It is *playfulness*. Queerness is experimenting. It is recognizing the Holy Spirit in our wildest imagination. It makes space for dress-up and acting, pulling out all the pots and pans, banging on the tops, and then running around the house, using them as superhero shields. It is trial and error; it is cannonballing into the waters of definitions of gender and sexuality, splashing water into the face of what is divine and human. It always tends toward a dynamic generosity, a grace that allows for mistakes and failures, because our lives are richer when we hold all of what is human.

Most important, it is *practice*. Queerness is an ethic. It is a decidedly intentional personal identity, but always, a social and political identity. It addresses the real world, the everyday, and all the struggles inherent inside and outside a person.

It is always an act of protest, a revolt, a demonstration, a rallying around people's humanity and dignity when larger institutions threaten it. It is advocacy. But more than an alliance, it is "allyship." That means accompanying people in their journeys through listening, respecting, confronting, standing with, confessing, and being responsible. It means showing up even if you don't get it or understand it or even agree with it. It means addressing all the bodily realities of people who are daily facing erasure and violence in all its forms—physical, structural, psychic, spiritual, and religious.

All these contexts matter to me, because they mattered to Jesus. Jesus the Christ, the carpenter from Galilee, was viewed as a radical and confronted traditions and institutions. He implicitly and organically lived, ministered, and died in such a way that he was grounded in his context as a first-century Jew yet challenged the racial, sexual, cultural, religious, and economic realities and more around him. He did so with a compelling fervor and creative brilliance, undoing the structures and systems with a mere parable or blessing, a touch or gesture. Finally, he himself was undone on the cross. Jesus acted queerly. Certainly, we could describe his actions as the dictionary definition of *queer,* "strange or odd from a conventional viewpoint; unusually different." Yet he doesn't merely act queer. He enacts and embodies queerness. Jesus *is* queer.

This is why queerness matters. This project is not so much about *making* Jesus queer but about seeing his queerness, to engage the presence and life of Jesus within the narratives of the biblical texts in provocatively faithful and intimate ways—ways that are fresh and open up the possibility of being. God, in Jesus, is oriented toward us in a queer and radical way. Through the life, work, and witness of Jesus, we see a God who loves us with a queer love. And our faith in that God becomes a queer spirituality—a spirituality that breaks boundaries and moves outside of the categories of our making.

Queerness matters. It is a matter of faith and a matter of spirituality. It matters to people who are trying to live but dying because of who they are and who they love. It matters to me as I struggle to orient myself in this world truthfully. It can matter to anyone, whether we identify with queerness or not, whether it resonates a little or a lot—because whenever we love ourselves and our neighbors with the boundary-breaking love of God, we enact this queer spirituality in the world.

Queerness matters because we need to see all the ways that we ourselves are loved by God, and loved in so many ways. And then we see and feel this in the myriad ways people love each other, which deepens and widens the very love of God in the world.

Notes

1. Janet E. Halley and Andrew Parker, *After Sex? On Writing since Queer Theory* (Durham, NC: Duke University Press, 2011).

1

On Fire for God

Thou hast made us for thyself, O Lord, and our heart is restless until it finds its rest in thee.

—Augustine of Hippo, *Confessions*

I have fallen in love many times.

The first time, I was in the second grade. The boy's name was Jason, and he had brown hair and brown eyes, asymmetrical dimples that flashed even when he wasn't smiling. A sprinkle of freckles splashed across his nose. We would say hi to each other first thing every morning and good-bye every afternoon as we stepped onto different school buses. Every time he spoke to me, I felt a little jolt, and dizzy, I would trip on the sidewalk.

One day he asked if he could be my boyfriend. I didn't know what that meant at the time, but I accepted, though nothing really changed in our daily routine. We didn't hold hands or share a kiss. We continued with our daily ritual of greeting each other in the morning and at the end of the day.

Then it was over. In fact, I can't even recall how our relationship officially ended. I have a feeling we both forgot and moved on.

Then I was in the fourth grade, and her name was Alicia. We had just moved to Denver, and I was a brand-new student at school. She lived in the same townhouse complex as my family, and after school and on the weekends, she would come over, or I would play at her house. She had short brown hair, feathered as was the style, and I admired the way it seemed so soft and shiny. She was *cool* in the way I understood it as an awkward nine-year-old with huge glasses and unruly hair barely tamed by ponytails. She always wore Reebok Pump high-tops with red shoelaces. I convinced my parents to buy me the exact same pair, except with blue shoelaces. Alicia was a natural artist, and we would spend hours drawing and painting, and she would encourage me in my own mediocre attempts.

As with Jason, we never held hands or shared a kiss. We stopped seeing each other when my family moved back to Colorado Springs the following summer.

Five years ago, I wouldn't have described Alicia as someone I had fallen in love with—maybe a best friend or a kind of sister. But I still remember the butterflies. They were the same butterflies I felt when Jason said good-bye to me every day. They were the same butterflies I felt when my husband, Andy, and I went on our first date and then later when we said our vows on our wedding day. Whenever Alicia stopped by in the mornings so we could walk to school together or when she spent the night, those butterflies always took a little flight in my belly. I remember that fluttery excitement was one I could barely contain. There was a chemistry, an energy and joy.

Those butterflies are powerful. They were—and are—so significant and universal that much has been written about them throughout history. Lengthy books and epic poems center on them. Songs and stories are full of the agony of unrequited love that sent whole countries to war on other shores. Families were torn apart in feuds lasting for generations because of their children's passion for each other. All because of these butterflies. For you, it may be butterflies, or it might be the feeling of riding on a roller coaster or waking up to Christmas morning every day or looking at the world through rose-colored glasses. There are a lot of ways to describe those butterflies. Sometimes even my stoic father would reminisce in a surprisingly goofy way about dating my mother: "Whenever I saw her, my heart would start pounding hard in my chest—ba-*boom*, ba-*boom*, ba-*boom*." These stories always made me laugh, but my mother would roll her eyes, embarrassed. Still, I would catch her smile, too; she just couldn't hide her pleasure at those memories.

I could recount numerous stories, as I imagine you might, too, about that feeling, that desire. While it can refer to wanting, needing, being desperate for some *thing*—some object, maybe a toy or shiny new iPhone or dark chocolate or that slice of pizza—it especially applies to desire for some *one*. However we describe the feeling of falling in love—whether it represents some semblance of intimacy, romance, or just even connection—it is powerful enough to prop up entire industries, including books, film, music, and even adult toy stores. This is the phenomenon that makes us alive. It makes us want to sing and shout from the rooftops or run for miles without stopping. Desire has an impact on our bodies. It quickens our hearts; it makes us heat up, with sweat on our foreheads, dripping down our necks, and off our clammy hands; it makes us light-headed and parches our throats. It motivates us, gets us up out of our beds, and drives us forward sometimes to connect, to explore and know, and if we're somehow lucky, to live and love.

Loving a Desiring God

When I was a college student, I was involved with an abnormally high number of Christian communities. I attended meetings for everything from Navigators to InterVarsity to the Presbyterian Campus Ministry to an Asian American ministry called Little Spark to Campus Crusade for Christ (now Cru). It seemed like many of the students around me picked one, maybe two of these as their primary community. But I just couldn't squeeze myself into one clique. I've never felt like I completely belonged anywhere.

The main group that gave me a way to do ministry as well as have meaningful friendships was Young Life, a nondenominational evangelical ministry to high-school and middle-school students led by college students. While some things in Young Life now give me pause, it gave me one of the most formative seasons in ministry and personal faith. It was one of the driving forces behind why I went into ministry. As nineteen- and twenty-year-olds being trained to do ministry with students a few years younger than us, we were encouraged to immerse ourselves in theology, that is, the language of our faith. A handful of books made the rounds in the group. Lovely spiritual memoirs by Brennan Manning, Bible studies on various books, and classic works including Oswald Chambers's *My Utmost for His Highest*—all these shaped my faith.

One popular book was John Piper's *Desiring God.* Honestly, I never fully read it. I pretended I did. When I finally got my hands on it after so many people raved about it, I was entering my senior year in college. Not only was I feeling senioritis and a little of the smug know-it-all attitude that comes with getting ready to graduate and take on the world, my head was stuffed with theories of religion. Philosophies and anthropologies. Social histories and cultural analysis of religion. Parts of my mind were awakening to some glimmering questions around race, gender, sexuality, and Christianity that I struggled to articulate, much less reconcile for myself. When I opened the book, the introduction suggested it would lead me back down a path that was too familiar, treading over paths that no longer seemed viable to me. Also, the book was substantial—it had way too many block quotes and long Scripture passages. So I halfheartedly skimmed it.

Desiring God is centered on the Westminster Shorter Catechism, which asks and answers, "What is the chief end of man? To glorify God and to enjoy him forever." This is one of the main confessions, or statements of faith, for those who belong to the Presbyterian faith. I cannot read this catechism without hearing the trembling voice of our sweet, old, white Sunday-school teacher. My immigrant church rented space from a dying white congregation, whose minister had passed away. My teacher was his widow. Every Sunday morning, she made our unruly group of second-generation Korean American children recite the first question and answer together as the opening to the lesson. But I never really gave much thought to the words—how glorifying God and enjoying God were connected.

You may have read *Desiring God*, or you may have never heard of it. Maybe like me, you disagree with the politics of John Piper. Either way, there is one idea I did glean from his notion of Christian hedonism: that enjoying God is a way to glorify God. In other words, pleasure and happiness are good, the longing for those things is universal and natural, desire is connected to joy (hence, hedonism), and the pursuit of pleasure is necessary for, as he writes, "worship and virtue."[1] Something like that, and yes, I got most of that from the introduction.

So, sure, okay, I can sign onto that. No emotionless stoicism or puritanical and confessional self-flagellation lifted up here. Experiencing pleasure is encouraged in our faith—or at least, pleasure in God, whatever that means.

I keep going back to the title. What if, instead of *desiring* being a verb, we read it as an adjective modifying and enhancing this image of God? A desiring God. A God who desires.

The Bible is replete with stories of a passionate God. In the Song of Songs or the Psalms, Hosea or Isaiah, we see that God loves intensely, obsessively and *wants* the people. God, newly in love and newly obsessed with a recently rescued but non-committal Israel, follows them throughout the desert, wooing them with milk and honey, cakes and delectable meats, but lashes out in hurt and anger when Israel chooses instead a powerless golden calf. God, desperate to prove a fiery love and devotion that will not be denied, showboats for Israel by drying up oceans, stopping rivers, and reducing the walls of cities to dust crumbles, only to catch Israel's eyes wandering time and time again. It is easy for us to imagine God's passion for us, God's longing and desire for us, in this way. God is really into the people of Israel.

On the flip side, we read in Scripture the ways God's people pine over God, whether it's in the Psalms or the prophets. From Psalm 18, one that I memorized as a high school student, come the following words of passion, words of an adoring people:

I love you, O Lord, my strength.
The Lord is my rock, my fortress, and my deliverer,
    my God, my rock in whom I take refuge,
    my shield, and the horn of my salvation, my stronghold.

Likewise, in the New Testament, Paul is trying to cohere his actions and passion for God, poured out in letters of love, to his fledgling churches all across the continent. Even today, we see similar expressions of desire for God in, for example, contemporary Christian songs or praise songs like "I Could Sing of Your Love Forever," a favorite of mine as a young person, and more recently, Chris Tomlin's "First Love," with lyrics about God as that first love and anchor and how God has won the singer's heart.

These could be songs by a boy band in the '90s or on *Billboard*'s Top 100. The tunes are catchy, and the words are easy. The images stoke a fire like the dramatic falling-head-over-heels of our youth. Anyone can listen; even a close friend of mine who is Jewish enjoys listening to the latest contemporary Christian hit on the radio. It's no wonder Christian radio stations have such far-reaching audiences, because while these images and words are suggestive in their own way, they remain PG—at most, PG-13. They take us to a safe puppy love. When we sing, talk, and imagine loving God in this way, we get to first, maybe second base. Our hearts are pounding hard in our chests, and our stomachs are aflutter with desire. This relationship with Jesus is akin to the steamy courtship in Jane Austen books.

Any inkling, the least possibility of rounding third base and getting to home, where sex is made analogous to the Divine Love, where we're thinking about God's desire to couple with humanity—this is heresy. It's sin and judgment. Yet the more I read about and understand God, the more I think, "God, we need a DTR [define the relationship]." There's so much more to the love of this God, who desires with the heat of a thousand suns.

Teresa of Avila, the famed sixteenth-century saint and mystic, understood this in her life. And she wasn't afraid to speak of it: "I saw an angel very near me, towards my left side, in bodily form. . . . He had in his hands a long golden dart; at the end of the point methought there was a little fire. *And I felt him thrust it several times through my heart in such a way that it passed through my very bowels.* And when he drew it out, methought it pulled them out with it and left me wholly on fire with a great love of God."[2]

To read something like this as a description of even a momentary connection with God flies in the face of our squeamish culture. Critics might reject Teresa's description of her love for God. They might question how she could even think about using this kind of language to describe her desire or God's desire for her. Or they might dilute it and overly spiritualize it to compensate for the carnal image. Whichever way you see her, Teresa deviates from our norms.

This language is deemed inappropriate because any expression of sex, whether it is erotic feeling, desire, act, or image, is taboo. It is antithetical to the experience of faith. Faith is pure and untouchable; it is intellectual, rational, and in essence cerebral. Sex is permissible only when contained within the structures of monogamy, within marriage, and even more specifically, within heterosexual marriage. So any deviance outside is abhorrent immorality and therefore susceptible to righteous judgment and disdain. Any participants or supporters are cast out where there will be weeping and gnashing of teeth.

As Christians, we've tended to demonize and vilify sex. But desiring God, wholly and fully, not only makes space for but inspires our pleasure. And then loving a *desiring* God is a fuller picture of a God who also yearns for our happiness, our joy, and yes, even our pleasure. To reiterate the Westminster Shorter Catechism, this is God's glory. To enjoy a gorgeous cityscape or breathe in a mountain scene or drink deeply from the sight of the ocean at sunset or a delectable meal and, yes, even physical intimacy with another person—all this suggests something divine and eternal.

A desiring God flips the world upside down. It's not about my desire for God; it's about God's desire for me. My faith is made all the more meaningful when I understand that God's love for me is like the passion of a lover who is hungry and thirsty for me. A desiring God is a game changer for someone like me who grew up straddling cultures that reject the body and tried to ignore the existence of the body's nerve endings. I was afraid of emotions, of feelings, especially when it came to pleasure. Thoughts of sexual pleasure made me feel shame.

A desiring God flips the world upside down for us. We might stand before a burning bush, wanting to grab our shoes and run, but love the feel of the heat of God's barely contained love. Sex and sexual desire are human experiences that are meant to expand our understanding of God's yearning for us, for that intimacy and connection with the whole world. God wants us, and this passion is irresistible.

Queering Desire

I finally gave in to desire when I was fourteen. My first kiss. His name was Jake. He was a crush from church, and oh, how my parents disapproved. He was mixed Asian, we were too young, and it was just "inappropriate," which fueled those flames even more and made us crazy for each other. When we finally kissed, it was like an unspoken promise. Even though it made me giddy, it felt oddly serious—and grown-up, too. It solidified the relationship. We were really and truly together. So, like any couple, we secretly passed letters during Sunday school, youth group, and any other church gathering. I felt a delicious queasiness every time he was near me. I began to dream about marrying him and later telling our children stories about how we were high-school sweethearts, like in the movies.

However, my parents found the letters and forbid me from interacting with Jake ever again. I cried for days and pined over him. I could hardly stand to see him at church, and like many woeful teenagers denied young love, I wrote lengthy, dramatic diary entries about the injustice of our separation. I thought about him every second of the day. I imagined what it would be like if he were different, if I were different, if my parents were different, and the world were different—if we could then have that happily-ever-after. Soon afterward, he moved away. I would hear snippets of news about him every once in a while. All those feelings faded away. The last I heard, he had been sent to a juvenile detention center and dropped out of school.

This wasn't the last time I felt the flames of desire. I went on to secretly date boys in high school then graduated to a couple of more serious long-term relationships in college with a sprinkling of hookups throughout it all. Each relationship and interaction was unique, but what united them was a constant feeling of total irrationality. There was drama, and it was always just way too over-the-top. Everything brimmed over with all the squishy and messy realities of bodies smashing into each other, literally and figuratively. The questions, the uncertainties, the analysis of feelings, and he-said or she-said always came as an afterthought to the physicality. Conversations were made complicated by the bodily experience of desire and the subsequent connections. But they were so intertwined that it was difficult to tease either out. Bottom line, I was mostly out of my mind.

Sometimes desire seemed to come from outside of me, or it seemed to emerge from somewhere deep within the center of my body. This possibility mystified me—feeling the same desire, the same desperation and obsession, the same struggle and complications for all these different people. But in many conversations with others, I've learned that I am not alone in this experience. What does this say about how we understand desire, intimacy, relationships, and ultimately, love?

Lauren Berlant, gender theorist and writer of the short yet dense book *Love/Desire*, initially suggests that love and desire are better understood as separate experiences. Desire is the attachment and the feeling of the possibility of the fulfillment of that connection. It contains the particular uniqueness of that object and all the promises, hopes, and dreams we project onto that attachment. In contrast, love is the result of that desire reciprocated by the other where that experience of connection expands your understanding of your self.

Yet, Berlant complicates this easy formula by exploring everything that surrounds love—the emotions and feelings, as well as the realities of power dynamics in relationships, the political issues surrounding monogamy and the institution of marriage, the role of family and property, and the impact of religious and cultural ideals. In other words, love and desire aren't so easily delineated. So rather than seeing love as an absolute or universal phenomenon, Berlant then proposes that the heart of the human experience is not love but desire.

Desire gives us a more authentic picture of who we are, and love is one way we know it and live it out. But, love, as we traditionally understand it, is fraught with conventions, rituals, traditions, and regulations.

When I was seven or eight years old, I saw a sticker that puzzled me. One of our church members had invited my family to a picnic on one of the military bases. There were hot dogs and hamburgers on the grill, and all the children were given glow sticks. I remember the hazy light of the sun setting and the lengthy dusk that typifies a Colorado summer. I wandered into one of the offices and over to a desk covered in stickers. One jumped out at me. It showed two stick figures—presumably male, since they didn't have the upside-down triangle shape of a dress. One figure was behind the other, and the front stick figure was bent over. Over the image was a large red circle with a line through it. My mother wandered in, and I pointed to the sticker and asked her what it meant. She glanced down and quickly pushed me out the door, saying, "We'll talk about it later."

When I asked about the sticker later, my mother and father said that men should not go with men, and women should not be with women. Doing so was against God and against natural creation. It was sin. I didn't question it any further.

When I was growing up, sex, desire, and intimacy were hardly talked about, whether in my home, at school, or at my church. I tried to make sense of it with the information I'd pieced together through random conversations, observations of pop culture, and the teachings of evangelical youth group and campus fellowships. Desire for a person was good only if this person could be "the one," with some vague notion of destiny. Then it was the work of trying to shove and contain it all within what I understood was the normative script for heterosexual marriage—courtship, engagement, marriage. We were taught this at a very early age with a children's song that was more like a taunt:

> Jane and John, sitting in a tree,
> K-I-S-S-I-N-G.
> First comes love, then comes marriage.
> Then comes the baby in a baby carriage.

As I continue to reflect on the relationship between desire and love, I see how the connection between what is expressed and lived out is never formulaic. These intimacies are not linear or straightforward, nor easily categorized.

I wonder what would have happened if I had let myself explore the butterflies I got from Alicia. I doubt that at age nine, I would have understood much beyond what our pre-pubescent imaginations allowed at the time, but there was never even the glimmering of a possibility.

This is where a desiring God throws open the doors to a room I had unknowingly closed off for so long. A desiring God makes space for all kinds of desire—queer desire. Queering desire means loosening the constraints around gender, sexuality, and sex. It gives us the beginning glimpses of all the variations of human feeling and expression. It unleashes all the prospects of deeper, wider, broader, fuller connection. This is a little what that brief moment in time with Alicia teaches me so many years later. A queer spirituality doesn't quench those flames, but fans them.

The Flames of Desire

In *Fire*,[3] Deepa Mehta's controversial, groundbreaking 1996 film, two middle-class women, Radha and Sita, are married to brothers but fall in love with each other. In the memorable ending of the film, one of the brothers, Ashok, walks in and catches the wives together, their arms and legs tangled up as they make love. In the kitchen the next day, Ashok angrily confronts Radha, blasting her with guilt: "What I saw in the bedroom was a sin against God and man." Before she can interrupt, he says, "Desire brings ruin," quoting Swamiji, a local preacher, his guru, who teaches the suppression of desires.

Radha, unable to control herself, fires back, "Without desire, I was dead. Without desire, there's no point in living. I desire to live. I desire Sita. I desire her warmth, her compassion, her body. I desire to live again."

Expressing desire itself and responding to desire are what lead Radha to see not only who she is but also how she can be fulfilled. And the verbal act of expression is what frees her. She could have left with Sita without waiting to speak this truth, but this declaration was a part of solidifying the reality of desire and her agency.

What a person desires tells the truth of the person's being. Desire frees us to see our innermost being, and that shines a light into the caverns of each person around us. When that desire is given space for expression, it allows humanity to expand outward, and the love that results is richer, fuller, and sweeter. When we are rooted in the queer love of God, all our existing boundaries dissolve—and these boundaries do not merely exist between people but are the kinds of lines drawn around people, marking off who we think we are or should be, and what that looks like. A desire rooted in flesh-and-blood bodies and intimacies in all their varied forms is an expression of faith in a God who originates and also reciprocates love, and that love is called out in its fullest expression in all our relationships. Queer intimacies are radical expressions of desire that open up traditional definitions and categories, and they invite us into understanding our humanity in new ways.

A queer spirituality challenges the compartments that we, not God, have created. A queer spirituality encourages us toward candid questioning what stirs our hearts. A queer spirituality urges us not to blindly accept what culture gives us but to interrogate it thoughtfully, wholeheartedly, and prayerfully. A queer spirituality welcomes desire. The butterflies we feel, the restlessness and longing, all have so much to tell us about ourselves. Even more so, they have something to tell us about a God who desires life and love for each of us.

Notes

1. John Piper, *Desiring God* (New York: Crown, 2011), 296.

2. Andrew Michael Flescher, *Heroes, Saints, and Ordinary Morality* (Washington, DC: Georgetown University Press, 2003), 176 (emphasis mine).

3. Deepa Mehta, Bobby Bedi, Shabana Azmi, Nandita Das, and Kulbhushan Kharbanda, *Fire*, collector's ed. (New York: New Yorker Video, 2000).

2

There Are No Girl Colors

It was not only colored people who praised John, since they could not, John felt, in any case really know; but white people also said it, in fact had said it first and said it still. It was when John was five years old and in the first grade that he was first noticed; and since he was noticed by an eye altogether alien and impersonal, he began to perceive, in wild uneasiness, his individual existence.

—James Baldwin, *Go Tell It on the Mountain*

Our kitchen is filled with all manner of children's supplies—sippy cups, plastic cutlery, and a half dozen small, white plastic bowls with blue or pink rims. We fill them up with cereal and pretzels, fruit and popcorn—basically, anything edible. Sometimes we find them around the house, serving as a bathtub for a Lego figure or a My Little Pony, or as a nest for a pile of flowers. I never followed the conventional rules of "pink is for girls and blue is for boys" with them. But at some point, out of nowhere, my children verbalized their demands for a specific color. I gave in very quickly.

Our boys—mostly Desmond, but his younger brother,

Ozzie, quickly followed suit—wanted the blue-rimmed bowls, protesting obnoxiously, as if the wrong color would curse them or curse their food. They threw full-on temper tantrums, so much so that I couldn't tell if there was something deeper going on: *Was he actually obsessed with the color, or was it the bowl itself?* Our daughter, Anna—twins with Desmond, but their birthday is really the only thing they have in common—gravitated to pink, arguing that "the color was pretty," and once, to my surprise, she said verbatim that pink is "for girls."

I finally put the kibosh on the color preferences, because I didn't want them to think in terms of *girls do this* and *boys do that*, as if there were limitations on their desires because of some arbitrary associations between gender and color. First it's gender and colors, then it's gender and toys, then clothes, then work, and suddenly a slippery slope loomed in front of me. Probably, I was overthinking it.

Really, it was just inconvenient. We didn't have enough bowls for them to always get their preferred color. Sometimes I purposefully gave pink bowls to the boys and a blue bowl to Anna, to mess with them a little. I did it because I don't want there to be colors, or anything, just for girls or just for boys. Now they hardly even notice the bowl, as long as there's food in it.

Identity is deeply important. It frames how we see, how we color, how we move and breathe through this world. It's a point of contact for others and the way we get under each other's skin and, eventually, connect to one another. But it's mediated by generations, economic systems, and cultural processes, and it's imposed upon us by social, familial, political expectations. Identity is clothes and gestures, language and eye shape, hair length and skin color, body shape and genitalia. Identity is reiterated through language and images, and then regulated by structures of power and ideology such as state agencies and religious institutions. We are all constantly negotiating our identities in relation to each other and to what is happening in the world, and this process takes place within the communities and networks we find ourselves. It's no wonder that we gravitate to colors to begin organizing human existence. Identity is so complex, and we have to start from somewhere.

And yet, the more I look around, it is clear a kind of revolution is happening around identity. People are recognizing the tenuous boundaries around their selves, whether it is the child who was assigned female at birth but verbalizes feeling like a boy, or the movement for black lives that resists violence against black bodies, or the Asian American woman who is regularly told that she is viewed as white by her white peers, who don't recognize that this effort to make sense of her existence becomes instead the cause of her erasure. It is happening as we see more and more representations of Jesus as other than the blue-eyed shepherd with flowy, shiny blond hair, creamy skin, and some kind of peach fuzz or goatee—images of him as an African man, as a man from the Middle East, as an Asian man, as a black man, and even as a woman.

British artist Edwina Sandys created a bronze statue named *Christa* that was briefly exhibited in the Cathedral Church of Saint John the Divine in New York City in 1984. It was installed on the altar in the Chapel of Saint Saviour, one of seven chapels in the ambulatory behind the choir. *Christa* was exhibited together with the work of twenty-one other contemporary artists, as part of a show called *The Christa Project: Manifesting Divine Bodies*. The show proposed to explore "the language, symbolism, art, and ritual associated with the historic concept of the Christ image and the divine as manifested in every person—across all genders, races, ethnicities, sexual orientations, and abilities."[1] What people saw was a threat to traditional imagery and a literal picture of Jesus we imagine we receive in the Scriptures. It was not only a mixing and mingling of the sacred and profane but jeopardized any stable view of their own humanity.

How we understand ourselves is constantly shifting, and it's that slippage that compels me. It's in that slippage where queerness emerges as a means to embrace the gray areas and the ambiguities. In this thin place, the miracle of strange but meaningful life emerges in spite of our lack of preparedness, and it changes us.

Identity Crisis: Who Am I?

When I think about identity, my mind turns immediately to race and gender—usually to race first, because of how it is experienced in the United States, especially for Asian Americans. More than half a century before World War II, several racial exclusionary laws affected those of Asian descent. They banned Asian men from becoming US citizens yet permitted using their labor in sugarcane plantations and their bodies to lay down railroads, while prohibiting marriage outside their race. The United States barred women from specific Asian countries, including India, China, and the Philippines. And then Executive Order 9066 led to the detainment in incarceration camps of those of Japanese descent. Finally, however, the 1965 Immigration and Nationality Act removed the national-origin quotas established in 1921, and the number of Asian immigrants grew from 491,000 in 1960 to about 12.8 million in 2014.

When my parents and I immigrated to the United States in the late 1970s with one of the major waves from South Korea, we took the traditional path to citizenship through naturalization. Seven years later, when I was eight years old, we were to be officially received, and I had the opportunity to change my name to an American name. At the time, it seemed many of the Korean Americans around us were adding a first name like Joanne, Christine, or Sarah, or David, Michael, or John. I don't remember exactly what I had picked; Rebecca (good biblical name) or Elizabeth (I liked all the possibilities of nicknames, which always struck me as solidly American).

Somehow we forgot the necessary paperwork or missed the deadline. Or maybe my parents got cold feet and didn't want me to change my name. Whatever the reason, the opportunity passed with no change in my name. I recall being disappointed, but the moment passed quickly, and I soon forgot about it.

That is, I forgot until the teasing began. At first, I was fielding questions about whether I was Chinese or Japanese. Then came the guesses, like a game: "Where did you come from?" Then there were all the variations and changes they made to Mihee, an easy target of a name. And since it's an Asian name, it was easily paired with ching-chong songs while my tormenters were pulling their eyes up at a slant: "Chinese, Japanese, dirty knees, look at these." These incidents led to years of propagating the deep shame a person can feel, calcifying that self-hatred until it becomes a part of one's skin and bones, which is almost what happened to me.

Actually, it did happen to me. When I got to college, I decided to finish the process we had begun at my naturalization. A few signed documents along with a certificate of naturalization and a Social Security card would do it. My official name became: Rachel Mihee Kim. Why Rachel? A few reasons: I didn't know many Korean Americans with that name, it was biblical (to appease my parents), and I'm embarrassed to say it, but I loved the show *Friends*.

The thing is, I hardly used my new name. Since I was still in the middle of college, I continued to go by Mihee with friends, acquaintances, and people in my program. The university had officially changed my name and given me a new email address, but even in class, whenever I was called on for attendance that first week, I asked to be called Mihee.

My new name was a useful mode of categorizing interactions with people.

I called Rachel my "Panera name." I would use it for convenience, like at restaurants or at Starbucks, because I could avoid the tedium of repeating my name at least a handful of times, spelling it, and explaining it, only to get the meal or the cup with my name spelled incorrectly, or yelled out incorrectly.

"MY-hee!"

"Miltee!"

"Mikey!"

I know. It's confusing with a name that uses two different vowels for the same vowel sound. I always had to explain it by reducing it to the familiar pronouns *me* and *he*. "Rachel" was helpful because it was effortless and uncomplicated to say. Except I still didn't really feel like a Rachel, and when I would give people that name, it felt false. I didn't have that confidence in my voice where you know yourself. Each time I used the name, I wondered if people could see through to my insecurity.

I started to give the name when, upon first impression, I decided I would likely not have any more conversations with a person—in other words, if I felt like I didn't like someone. It was a way to separate out people I would know in a very casual way from the people I thought I would eventually befriend. And then I got married and hyphenated my last name with Andy's, and all of a sudden, I had too many names. When I signed up for anything, like at the doctor's office or at a hair salon, I couldn't remember which name I had used on the forms. I'd have to give them all the variations on my name as they looked at me askance: Rachel Kim-Kort? Rachel Kort? Mihee Kim-Kort? Mihee Kort? *Don't you know your own name?* Then to be in a scenario where I was with a mix of some people who knew me as Rachel and others who knew me as Mihee—well, that was awkward, to say the least. I felt strange, like a fraud.

This is what we might call an identity crisis.

The orthodox view of identity is that the individual self is somehow autonomous and independent of external sources—that there is something natural, pure, and untouched (and untouchable) by outside forces of socialization. Other psychologists believe a person comes to their identity through internalizing the influence of certain people, specifically one's mother and/or father. Each human being is an amalgamation of the people who would have the most influence, a combination of genetic and personality traits. Identity is a symbiotic process between the individual and the community.

The process is never linear, but full of ebbs and flows. An "identity crisis" can occur when a person feels disconnected from the community that gave the person their identity. This creates a fissure in the person's self-understanding and self-expression. I can point to a number of times throughout my life when I experienced an identity crisis of sorts, and race and gender were always both wrapped up in it.

Of course, this is not uncommon. We all experience moments in our lives that precipitate crises of identity. For me, these happened in college, trying to understand myself in relation to others; in seminary, trying to understand and engage my faith; in marriage, trying to live out this covenantal relationship; and in becoming a minister, in becoming a mother, more recently in becoming a Midwesterner, and more. When I look back, I can hardly see an extended period of time when there was no crisis concerning my identity, whether it was getting my period or rebelling against being the hardworking Asian student. In fact, I can say with all honesty that I struggled throughout most of my life to name myself, to know myself, to recognize myself when I looked in the mirror.

But every single time, when I felt on the point of total and utter despair, it was community, a gathering of others, a tribe who would raise me out of that cavernous hole of existential anguish, whether it was too many voices trying to tell me who I am or the absence of a voice within me. It was the realization that my identity wasn't completely internal and innate, but that the people around me who love me hold up mirrors for me to see myself more clearly. Each time, they would call me out of that abyss by baptizing me in an ocean of love and hope: naming me beloved, adventurer, child of God, sister, wild and holy.

Naming: I Am Who I Am

Names—whether Rachel or Mihee or even pastor, mother, student, writer—are not meant to be exhaustive of who a person is. We get caught up in names because we see them as a way to extend ourselves, to know and be known, fully and completely. When I took on Rachel as my legal first name, it was a way of saying, "I'm one of you." It was my way of saying, "I'm human. I'm like you." But that's not how it works. Even when I gave my name as Rachel, people would often show shock and surprise when they heard me speak perfect English or tell them I was from Colorado.

Did I expect my name to signal something clear to the world? Names matter only if we believe they point us to some coherent and absolute sense of self, and that this sense of self can be captured in this thing called identity, which we try to express through labels and categories. In Scripture, we read that Moses encountered God in the wilderness engulfing a tree in flames without totally consuming it. God identifies God's self as the "God of your father, the God of Abraham, the God of Isaac, and the God of Jacob" (Exodus 3:6).

Of course, Moses asked God to prove God's self, and it was a sly way to say, "What am I supposed to tell the people when they ask who sent me?" And then God offered something vaguely . . . definitive: I am who I am (Exodus 3:14).

Perhaps what is more truthful is not that we are meant to have this system of consistent desires and steady ambitions, as if each person is a metaphysical being, totally aware of oneself at all times—unless, maybe, the person is a guru or bodhisattva, a being that has attained enlightenment. We are all an amalgamation of stories and dreams, histories and genetics, easily affected by lunar cycles, barometric pressure, and sunshine. We're made of stardust, and each of us is a complicated mashup of ancestors, cultures, ideologies, and time period. We are created in the image of the one who is named "I am who I am," and somehow we are called to the same work of creation, of imagining, of redeeming, of calling out, of sanctifying, of living and moving throughout this world.

Naming is more helpfully understood as descriptive rather than defining. In Genesis 1–3, we're able to read two accounts of creation. For six days, God worked obsessively, an artist consumed with every meticulous detail, every blade of grass; every molecule of water; all colors, shapes, and sizes; every claw and fingernail; every gill and nostril of every single creature; every glittery planet in the sky. Then God made *ha-'adam*. God gave *ha-'adam* dominion over all creation and empowered the earth creature to name all things in existence. In doing so, God bound creation to humanity and made humanity a co-creator with God. Naming is powerful but such a responsibility. Biblical theologian Phyllis Trible gives us a compelling reinterpretation of a passage normally cited for traditional, patriarchal roles and gender categories. She writes that this creature need not necessarily be thought of as male. Rather, the Hebrew text presents us with a wordplay: *ha-'adam* ("earth creature") is created from the earth, *ha-'adamah*.[2]

This earth creature remains without identity—sexless and

genderless—until the distinction of female from male occurs in Genesis 2:21-23. When the second creature is formed by *ha-'adam*'s rib cage, it is as an '*ezer k-negdo*—an expression that in English is translated as "helper" or "helpmate," even though the Hebrew doesn't carry any domestic or demeaning nuances. The sense of '*ezer* is expressed better by the phrase "a companion corresponding to it." The kind of naming that happens here is distinct from the naming *ha-'adam* enacts over all creation. Eve, as Adam's companion, is partner in mutuality, equality, solidarity. Eve is less derivation and more differentiation. This changes the way we have traditionally identified her, which was "helper" and, yes, weaker, lesser, originator of sin. This change in naming is life-giving for women, certainly, but for all of humanity, too, shifting all those relationships.

In other words, we call each other into new life when we are given the power to name each other. Yet that power is often wielded to hurt, to decimate, to erase, to cause life to shrivel up, especially when the naming is not true, when the naming is rooted in greed, when the naming is connected to oppression and destruction. Savage. Foreigner. Three-fifths. Illegal. Second-class. Sometimes naming is problematic, when we demand that people make an account of themselves, to explain and legitimize their existence.

Naming is a gift, a privilege. It becomes a special responsibility for all when we use it as a means to relate to and understand one another.

So the work of naming, when enacted genuinely, is sanctifying. It's calling out, it's lifting up, and in that work, it's resurrecting. Jesus calls Lazarus, brother of Martha and Mary, out of the grave after four days, after a stench began to seep out between the cracks of the tomb. Jesus calls him by name, calls him to new life. Jesus gives life, life-back and life-again, to the little girl who lay dead in her cot, to blind Bar-Timeus, whose days were wasting away on the side of the road, and to the woman hemorrhaging blood. He gives life to the lepers, to the hungry, to the possessed, to the tax collectors and sex workers, and to lowly fishermen.

Then when Jesus calls the first disciples, he calls Simon something new: Cephas in Aramaic (Peter in the Greek), meaning "rock." Today, Peter is a common name, but it was originally a nondescript, ordinary name, like naming someone Tree or Cloud. This kind of renaming is actually common throughout the Bible. All throughout the Scriptures, we see this tradition in which a new name signals a new reality: Abram becomes Abraham, Sarai becomes Sarah, Jacob becomes Israel, and Saul becomes Paul. Simon becomes Peter, and it's truly fitting, since throughout the rest of his time with Jesus, he appears to have the intelligence of a rock. He is not quite the cornerstone that he later becomes to the early church.

Still, Jesus names him Peter—not Rock-Head, Knuckle-head, or Future Cornerstone, but Peter, simply the rock, as if it were less a prophecy and more of a promise. It was a promise, though, not about *his* life (as in Peter would have a life of smooth sailing) but that God was already his rock. God was his foundation. Jesus loved him and named him, and that relationship meant something. It was sealed by the name. No explanations were necessary; no definitions, no labels mattered as much as the promise of God's steadfast love to him.

That's the kind of identity that resonates with me—an identity that is an invitation, a beckoning into freedom. An identity that is a call into being one who is loved. That conception of identity is a gateway into connection and communion, is space wide enough for me—for us—to play, to live, to breathe.

Queering Recognition

Identity isn't lived out in a vacuum. It's never as simple as just saying, "I am who I am." Identity is affected by things external to us and things internal. Identity is tricky in the way it attempts to cast who we are in categories like gender, race, and sexuality. Gender constrains us, but *queer* is the open mesh of possibilities with gaps and overlaps, dissonances and resonances, lapses and excesses of meaning.[3] Identity is better engaged as the spaces all around the boxes we check off—Korean, Christian, woman, spouse, mother.

Names are how we maneuver in and through all those containers of identity and occupy the fissures between them. Identity is a way we know and are known in relationship, and the names and labels we take on can help root us in our identities. At the same time, queerness can help us embrace the fluidity of our identities and the multiple points of connection. Queering our experience of identity involves a sense of playfulness and openness to the unknown. Not-knowing isn't laziness or willful ignorance but a trusting in, as queer theorist Eve Sedgewick says, "possibility without result," regarding all inklings and glimmerings as connected to the full picture.

Early in the 2015 biographical film *The Danish Girl*,[4] which is based loosely on the lives of married Danish painters, Gerda Wegner asks her husband, Einar, to stand in for a female model who is late to pose for a painting Gerda is working on. This act awakens something in him, and we can easily witness the struggle on his face as he fingers the beautiful dress draped across his body. Throughout the rest of the film, rather than fighting this identity, he embraces it by taking the name Lili. He begins a love affair with a man named Henrik. In one scene, Lili sneaks off to Henrik's apartment, and Henrik asks Lili why she hasn't talked to Gerda, who Lili pretends is her cousin, about them. He tells Lili, "I don't like all these lies."

Lili responds evasively, "She's very protective."

"Why don't you just tell her about us?" Henrik asks again.

Lili says, "I couldn't do that," to which Henrik looks visibly frustrated.

Lili is quiet, and Henrik tries to comfort her and make amends. "Sorry, I don't mean to upset you." They begin to kiss, and as it becomes more intimate, Henrik whispers, "Einar," and that catches Lili off guard. She looks at him and says, "What?" upset that Henrik knows she is Einar yet still seems to want to be with her. "Come on, it's all right," Henrik says.

"I don't understand," says Lili. "I don't know what you want. I don't know what you mean."

Henrik responds, "I want you," and Lili says, forcefully, "No." She pushes him away and runs out of the apartment, stopping twice to look at her reflection in storefront windows on her way home.

Einar is on the cusp of fully embracing Lili. It's affirmed by the external world in the person of Henrik, a potentially intimate partner who would consummate the transformation, if Lili allowed for it. But when Henrik says the name "Einar" aloud, it shatters the illusion. The reality she felt emerging in herself became little more than fantasy, a reflection and image. This throws her world into turmoil. Alone, she sees Lili, she feels Lili, she is Lili, but it is in her relationships with Gerda, with Henrik, and with others that she has to intentionally cultivate that identity. She narrows the possibility of romance and love to one experience, and when it is wrecked by Henrik's attempt to fully recognize and receive her—her history and her present struggle—she has to shift her orientation not only to him but also to her own self.

We can create, we can discover, and we can know ourselves, but we live in a world where others also answer the question of who we are. This shapes us, but when identity is experienced in terms of desire and love, we can choose to let it shatter our world or expand it beyond our imagination.

I see identity as a continuum. Dr. Alfred Kinsey developed

a scale to describe a person's sexual orientation based on their experience or response at a given time.[5] The scale typically ranges from 0, meaning exclusively heterosexual, to 6, meaning exclusively homosexual. I find myself comfortable on that spectrum.

But the spectrum isn't the only way to define myself, and if I would choose a specific designation, it would likely be close to bisexual. Imagine the reality of identity as the meeting point of all different Kinsey scales. Queerness engages those measurements—but also liberates us from them, because queerness acknowledges that identity cannot be so easily defined or categorized. In disrupting traditional categories around identity, queerness liberates us from the constraints of being named, of being defined by a container or a cabinet full of bowls stacked neatly on top of each other. A queer spirituality allows for loving pandemonium—the challenge of shifts and transitions, the realization that we are shaped by each other, and the emergence of new identities, new creations within each relationship.

***

The name Mihee was given to me by my paternal grandfather, and it is a common Korean name. It means "beautiful girl," and today that is the name I give to anyone and everyone, spelling it out loudly and clearly, and explaining, when asked, that it is Korean. I'm done trying to pass—to fit into the boxes for what is considered legitimate or real—for white or

Korean or woman or mother or whatever. I want to simply be.

I am who I am.

Because of my own history, my parents, my family, the social conditions in which I grew up, yes, but also because of the mysterious grace of God that binds it all together in love in this body, mind, and spirit.

I give my name to the cashier at Starbucks and then glance up at the bulletin board above the milk station. A Race for the Cure poster urges, "Be more than pink."

I stare at those words, thinking about Anna in her pink bike helmet and pink KangaROOS shoes easily racing past the boys on her pink bike. Anna and her dolls and My Little Ponies, Anna with her yellow jump rope with the pink handles, Anna in the summer always with flowers. She is more than pink, but even so, she wears it well.

Notes

1. Cathedral Church of Saint John the Divine, "Programs: The Christa Project," n.d., https://tinyurl.com/y9tda6c8.

2. Phyllis Trible, *God and the Rhetoric of Sexuality* (Philadelphia: Fortress Press, 1978), 80.

3. Eve Sedgewick, *Epistemology of the Closet* (Berkeley: University of California Press, 1990), introduction.

4. *The Danish Girl*, directed by Tom Hooper (Focus Features, 2016).

5. This is found in and elaborated on in the Kinsey Reports, included in two books on human sexual behavior, *Sexual Behavior in the Human Male* (Philadelphia: W. B. Saunders, 1948) and *Sexual Behavior in the Human Female* (Philadelphia: W. B. Saunders, 1953). This language also is used on the Kinsey Institute website, https://tinyurl.com/ydz83d6q.

3

Blessed Are the Promiscuous

Attraction is simply more nuanced for more people than some of us want to admit, sometimes even to ourselves. That attraction may never manifest as physical intimacy, nor does it have to, but denying that it exists creates a false, naïve and ultimately destructive sense of what is normal and possible. . . . Different people can experience attraction differently. For some, the order of attraction starts with body first. That's fine. For others though, it starts with the being first, the human being, regardless of the body and its gender.
—Charles M. Blow, *Fire Shut Up in My Bones*

In 2006, Canadian singer Nelly Furtado released a catchy earworm called "Promiscuous," from her third studio album, *Loose*, featuring Timbaland. Mixing with R&B sounds and a hip-hop vibe, the album wandered down a different road from her first album with hit songs like "I'm Like a Bird," which was a much more upbeat pop song. "Promiscuous" felt like something straight out of a club and had an after-midnight tone to it—mysterious, illicit, and seductive. When you hear those first beats and Furtado singing the refrain in a throaty way, as if she were caught in a moment of elation, it's hard to resist dancing and moving, too.

When I was growing up, expressions of sex, desire, or fantasy—whether found in music, literature, images, or art—were framed in a language of hiddenness, with undertones of shame and guilt, and not just in church but in school, too. That old adage "sex sells" is correct and isn't limited to overt sexuality. Suggestive, titillating, and implicit sex sells, too, and maybe even more so. And then, of course, there were the overly medicalized sex-education classes, which were taught in a way meant to diminish the strangeness of sex but actually reinforced its taboo.

In a scene in one of my all-time favorite movies, *Mean Girls*,[1] Coach Carr teaches a health class on sex. He opens with, "Don't have sex, because you will get pregnant and die! Don't have sex in the missionary position, don't have sex standing up, just don't do it, okay, promise?" And then he pulls out a box and says, "Okay, now everybody take some rubbers."

The parody hits the mark. My parents never talked about sex and sexuality with me; I used to joke that I got off lucky. I generally understood the basic mechanics around reproduction, and I knew what it's like to carry a pretend baby (read: an egg or a bag of flour) around for a month. But I didn't understand how sex, sexuality, desire, and identity are intertwined. That repression affected me in a significant way, like cutting off an appendage. Something was missing, and it crippled my sense of self.

Being closed off in this way meant I could never fully connect with others. I feared attraction and those more carnal desires, feeling that any sort of intimate connection was related to sex. But queerness undoes these rigid structures and boundaries. Radical love dissolves borders between people and eradicates the binary.[2]

Embracing an identity as a "promiscuous people"[3] is a way of living into this radical love.

Promiscuity is characterized by many transient sexual relationships, and we can psychologize and pathologize all the reasons people are promiscuous. It is associated with not only disease but also immorality. Multiple sexual partners indicates a lack of faithfulness, and it challenges the monogamous structures of marriage and the basic family unit. For this reason, among many others, it is often used to debase the queer community. But the word promiscuous means more. It is rooted in the Latin word for "to mix" and carries with it a sense of bringing together various elements. This notion of promiscuity as indiscriminate mingling is a far cry from the negative cultural definition of promiscuous we use in a more judgmental way. The global leader for the Metropolitan Community Churches, Rev. Dr. Nancy Wilson, draws on this definition of promiscuous in what she calls queer people's penchant for "promiscuous hospitality." It's an orientation outward toward others, and particularly the Other, to see and love with the indiscriminate excess of divine love.

I've got a tangled history with this excess.

During the summer of 2000, I had multiple sexual partners.

After I graduated from college, I decided that I needed to get out of Dodge, so I moved to a small college town on the East Coast for a few months. I worked some random jobs, traveled a little, and ended up partying . . . a lot. I went home with a different guy, or girl, nearly every weekend, and it became almost a ritual, a habit—not only something to do, but almost a conquest of sorts, a tallying up.

I was struggling on a few fronts: angst about graduating from college, confusion about body image, and most of all, a desire to extricate myself from a relationship back home. But instead of doing it in a grown-up way, I decided to self-sabotage. In the desire to cut myself off from any and all relationships, including one with God, I filled that void with these one-night stands. I was empty. Eventually I realized I was shriveling up on the inside and needed to come back to life. So, I did, I stopped numbing myself and took the first step—I got tested. By some strange and unknown miracle, the results came back clear. I went back home to Colorado, and began to heal.

For a long while, my sexual history was something I kept hidden because of the judgement of promiscuity. There was shame—shame about defaulting on virginity and purity, and then disgust with, I think, what I perceived as lack of control or morality. Though I still wrestle with that backstory in my life today, the conflict when it arises within myself is less about the multiple sexual partners and more about how I closed myself off from love. What I did was certainly irresponsible and risky, and in the end, it was not life-giving.

But queerness has helped me redeem this story in a way that's meaningful for my life. A queer spirituality reminds me that beneath any struggle and story is a desire to love and be loved, and to love extravagantly and capaciously—to love without holding back.

Beneath this story is also a desire to love well by making space for others to be filled up. I'm not an expert in hospitality, but to make space for others is core to who I am. Hospitality is ingrained in our culture: think everything from service industries to hospitals and hotels. It's deeply embedded within Christianity as well, in everything from doilies for tea, to lemonade on the lawn after church services, to putting out name tags for visitors. But, queering hospitality means thinking beyond concepts of "welcome" and "inclusion," so that people are not simply objects of certain outreach programs, additive and supplemental to our community.

Queering hospitality blows the doors wide open in human interaction; it's not selective or methodical but a table overflowing. Hospitality is a continuous recognition of another's humanity, and simultaneously, it's a loving solidarity with that person. Further, it is seeing not only the humanity of the person in front of us but our own humanity, too.

Beyond Welcome

It's easier to be hospitable to those who fit our categories. It's easier if the person looks like us, walks and talks like us, and smells like us.

Jesus encounters a Samaritan woman in John 4, and my

reading of and reflection on this story for a long time has lately sparked much of what I believe about queerness. It made me see myself differently because of the way the Samaritan woman saw Jesus, the way Jesus saw her, and the way she saw herself.

The Gospel tells us that while Jesus makes his way from Judea to Galilee, he stops at Jacob's well in a Samaritan city called Sychar. Jesus is tired out by his journey, and when a woman approaches the well, he asks her for some water. From there, they have a conversation about living and eternal water, and as usual, Jesus reveals some things about her life to her, and about who he is, too.

When Jesus sits down and converses so casually with the Samaritan woman, she doesn't pull any punches. Jesus's dialogue with her is unlike anything anyone has heard and seen, and even today, it is still provocative. We don't totally know her backstory, but we tend to make pretty unfair assumptions about her sexuality and relationships. Nevertheless, she is complex and fascinating, and her interaction with Jesus wreaks havoc on all those seemingly impervious structures around us that tell us what's proper. Their exchange makes us question everything we know about what's appropriate. It's an expansive, generous text with so much to traverse.

When Jesus asks the woman for a drink of water, she responds with a question: "How is it that you, a Jew, ask a drink of me, a woman of Samaria?" (John 4:9). It's an astonishing, brash question, but completely legitimate. Jesus is shirking the convention of his society by not only speaking to her but also requesting help from her—first, a Samaritan. Then, a woman. It's common knowledge that Jews and Samaritans have a history of hating each other, dating back to when Israel was divided into two kingdoms. The Samaritans inhabited the former northern kingdom, and the Jews inhabited the former southern kingdom, and both groups detested one another.

For 550 years, walls of bitterness were erected on both sides. They fought over who had the rightful lineage. They battled over who had the correct place of worship. All these walls became institutions and structures grafted into the identities of every individual in the community. How people should interact with one another was determined by age, gender, socioeconomic class. A Jew wouldn't have even glanced in the direction of a Samaritan. Yet here is a disruption. A fissure appears in the foundation of those systems that said who to talk to, who to interact with, and how.

I wonder how Jesus was able to ignore the ideological currents of hatred, prejudice, and misogyny that coursed through the veins of his people and hers. Somehow Jesus speaks to the Samaritan woman so freely. But then the audacity of the Samaritan woman responding to him is equally remarkable. Traditional interpretations will simply claim the divinity of Jesus as the reason for his unusual actions. While Jesus's divinity and his legitimacy as the Messiah are clearly perpetual themes running throughout the Gospel of John, perhaps we might more carefully occupy the possibilities in this space where the Samaritan woman encounters Jesus at the furthest edges and outskirts of the narrative—this space of intermingling.

Then Jesus says to her, "Give me a drink." For me, this is the revelatory moment, because the request shreds rules and convention. In addressing the Samaritan woman, Jesus chooses to disidentify with his Jewishness and his maleness. Disidentifying becomes a strategy of transformation and resistance.[4] It is another aspect of the blessedness of promiscuity. It doesn't necessarily mean to completely shed one's identity; that's almost impossible. Though Jesus seems to reject those societal norms, he remains a first-century Palestinian Jewish man. He is a regular participant in synagogue life. He observes the Sabbath and other important festivals and holy days. He partakes in community life, attending dinners and weddings.

This capacity to work on and against the ideological structures that would normally prohibit their interaction is part of the core of Jesus's queerness. Rather than succumbing to these expectations, he disidentifies with the powers that dictate who, what, when, how, and where he interacts with others. Queerness is an essential part of Jesus's identity and of the way he reconciles divinity and humanity within himself. Queerness is a means of resistance that isn't passive but constructive. Though queerness fragments, it is constitutive; it is the beautiful, creative power of the *logos*, the word becoming flesh.

In opening himself up to the Samaritan woman, he constructs a new identity and critiques the identities imposed on him by the empire, even as he is fully rooted himself. He is the Son of God engaging a human being. He is a rabbi and prophet, and he is also a needy person. He is a person with desires. He is a Jewish person addressing a Samaritan, but he is also a Jewish man engaging a Samaritan woman.

At its heart, queerness is promiscuous. It makes space for mixing and mingling, and for multiple identities to exist at once. It invites creative identity making and connection in every moment. Identity is fluid in that boundaries are porous, so interactions possess the potential of that slippage at any moment—as in this moment between Jesus and the Samaritan woman.

Jesus's complicated identity shows us a path toward queer welcome. Queering welcome is an invitation to call into question what identity is—how we use it to limit and restrict, welcome and reject people. It destabilizes and refashions identities not as strict categories but as multiplicities and sub-jectivities. It unmakes and remakes psyches. It has impacts on the subconscious and consciousness. It undermines the larger systems and inserts itself into the struggle within ordinary, everyday conflicts.

Jesus's request for help is more than an invitation; it is a rupture, a rending, an opening. The woman responds, "How is it that you, a Jew, ask a drink of me, a woman of Samaria?" She points out his identity and names her own; reminds him of convention, of history and tradition; questions him; criti-cizes him; and judges him. While the Samaritan woman has a choice simply to respond to Jesus by giving him what he requested of her, she recognizes what Jesus is doing here and calls it out. It flies in the face of what's normal and normative, and she tries to make sense of it as the structures of propriety begin to crumble around her.

She names the problems in this exchange, and the clash of identities. In doing so, she also participates in the process of disidentification, shifting everything beneath her feet—and his feet, too. He responds, "If you knew the gift of God, and who it is that is saying to you, 'Give me a drink,' you would have asked him, and he would have given you living water" (John 4:10).

I imagine Jesus watching the wheels turn in her head: He asks for a drink. Then offers me a drink? Perhaps he has had a touch of sun. She ponders this for a moment. This man is making strange statements, and then he's got the audacity to offer me water when he clearly has no jar? She speaks again. "Sir, you have no bucket, and the well is deep," she observes. "Where do you get that living water? Are you greater than our ancestor Jacob, who gave us the well, and with his sons and his flocks drank from it?"

She keeps at it. Perhaps she senses the possibility of a deeper truth in this queer interaction; in a way, she is thirsty for it. This encounter with Jesus has suddenly awakened a thirst she never knew she had before.

In this moment, Jesus and the Samaritan woman are culturally at odds, but a new kind of connection occurs. Without promiscuous searching and a willingness to engage beyond one's borders, this connection would be impossible. But it's not only the way they engage each other; it's also how we engage Jesus, and how we engage the Samaritan woman. We might read slight belligerence in her question but also a surprising curiosity by a woman who would not normally participate in that level of engagement. There is a bubbling intelligence, and a sign of thriving life here despite her circumstances. In this interaction, we see the possibility of reading both the woman and Jesus differently.

When she questions Jesus, they make and remake the world with the fragments of identity that lay strewn around them. The well is a place where her ancestors worshipped, and it is a tangible object that informs her identity. But waters there will run dry someday, and the conversation with Jesus has opened up the occasion in which she might find eternal life—her life, her being—specifically, in this scandalous relationship with Jesus. What is promiscuous about this moment is the radical mixing and crossing of boundaries, not only between Jesus and the Samaritan woman, but also those around their individual lives.

Queering Hospitality

This Jesus shapes my continuous reflection about solidarity and hospitality—how they go hand in hand. Truly, blessed are the promiscuous, because they reify this kind of connection, this reaching out and across lines to see and recognize another's humanity. They notice something familiar in the stranger.

I often think that both Jesus and Mr. Rogers were on to

something when they constantly talked about how we can be a neighbor. It's deeply and radically embodied; it's skin and bones, flesh and blood. We need to remember to see ourselves and others as embodied, especially those lives and bodies that are particularly vulnerable. This is at the heart of the Christian faith, to love my neighbor as myself, including love of what is traditionally categorized—whether by policy or prejudice, ideology or theology—as foreign, other, alien, or stranger. And then, even more strange—and queer—love extends to those who are deemed my enemy, that is, those who hate me. It means, then, that we do not see anyone as a stranger or foreigner or outsider or enemy; every human being shares our humanity. Every human being is our neighbor.

When I think of hospitality, I often go to the story of another Samaritan, the story told by Jesus in response to the question of who is my neighbor. It might seem innocent, but a queer spirituality reads this question as suggestive. It's expansive. It's the kind of question that begs promiscuity, for the reader to entertain being stretched beyond our usual answers.

When I sit outside on our porch and look out on our world—blue skies and birds, the laughter of all the neighborhood kids, ringing bells on bikes—I feel all its odd and discomforting tranquility. I watch my children play in dirt, plucking flowers, transplanting insects to old mason jars. I look at the houses around me on our street, the homes of our neighbors. And this is the question from the parable of the

Good Samaritan that always, always leaps out at me: Who is my neighbor?

I have an icon at home from the Taizé community, which I visited for the first time in 2016. The icon depicts the parable of the good Samaritan in six small circular panels around the image of Christ. It was commissioned by the brothers and inspired by their community focus that year: the courage of mercy. I meditate on the icon often during the few moments of quiet I find here and there. I linger on the various panels, which illustrate the story: the two robbers' hands; the two religious leaders, who are praying with eyes upward, standing above the man, who is now lying on the ground; the Samaritan picking up the robbed man to place him on his donkey; the Samaritan carrying him into the hotel; the Samaritan caring for the man's wounds; and in the final image, the Samaritan, the now-restored man, and a third man, presumably the innkeeper, gathered around a table for a meal.

That last panel catches my eye as it reminds me of another icon, one of the Trinity I saw once at a church. Both have three people sitting around a table, and there's a large bowl or chalice in the middle of the table. And it strikes me that there's a deliberate connection between the restoration of a human being to community and the very communal nature of the Triune God. A queer spirituality views the Trinity as an expression of promiscuous hospitality, and it is a glimpse of the kingdom that when we pursue mercy to its end, it will always result in the full restoration of every single human being to the wider human community.

I pondered this after weeks of violence and death. Two black men and five Latinos were killed by police.[5] Dallas, where a military veteran—unassociated with a protest against police brutality—killed five police officers and injured more. Terrorist attacks abroad in Istanbul and Baghdad tragically disrupted a holy season for our Muslim brothers and sisters. Flint, Michigan, continued to be without drinkable water, and at Standing Rock, the Sioux tribe and other supporters were fighting against the pillaging of this land. The Orlando massacre and the memory of a vigil full of tears, rainbow flags, and bubbles were still fresh in my mind.

Who is my neighbor? This question isn't only about whom we are a neighbor to, and who is a neighbor to us. A queer spirituality challenges us to think about what it means to live in this world together by recognizing the plurality of the question. This neighbor question must take into account the reality that we have systems and institutions that permit these tragedies—the killing of black and brown bodies, refugee children, LGBTQIA persons, and police officers—to occur on a regular basis. We won't experience true healing and reconciliation until we reform those structures so that all are free and equal, and this won't happen unless we are willing to cross over and connect with those normally out of our social radius.

Who is my neighbor? Addressing that question is a working out, a continuous process of waking up to the people around you, and drawing near to them in the same way God draws near to us. God draws near to us over and over in the most unexpected ways, using the least likely places and faces—maybe in ditches or on roads, even on freeways. Addressing Who is my neighbor? means to live as if we belong to each other, to live as if we need each other, because we do. We aren't going to survive for much longer on the road we're barreling down. Addressing Who is my neighbor? looks like choosing joy and then choosing to love harder, love stubbornly, love persistently, love promiscuously, so that neighbor looks more like kinfolk and family.

I haven't yet talked about any of the recent tragedies with my children. There are too many to count these days. But if there is a vigil in the near future, I do expect to attend with them. Because if there's anything I believe about following Christ (the one who is about solidarity and hospitality, the Christ of the Triune God), it's that we keep showing up. Who is my neighbor? is a question that we keep trying to answer by going out and showing up in body, mind, and spirit. A promiscuous hospitality asks of us our whole selves. Even when we don't understand, even when we are guilty or complicit or fragile or confused, even when it doesn't make sense, even when we are despairing, we show up to be with people: to pray, to light candles, to hold hands, to chant "Black lives matter," to whisper "God, have mercy."

Transgressing Boundaries

I've spent some time at a community of mercy called Shalom Community Center in Bloomington, Indiana. To get there, I have to cross a busy street. Each time, I pause, waiting for the crowd of cars to dissipate a little, so I can quickly scootch across, hands in my jacket pockets. Looking across the way, I see that many of the struggling and displaced clients are milling around outside. Some are laughing raucously at a joke while playfully shoving each other. Some are standing and staring off into the distance. The weather is frigid, so I can see their breath making wisps of clouds around them. Those clouds contain cigarette smoke, too. Some clients are walking into the building, hunched over, carrying huge packs on their backs and old grocery bags in their arms.

I take a deep breath and cross, squeak out a "Good morning" to some people outside, and walk to the door. When I enter the building, my glasses steam up. Some folks look up at me, curious and inquisitive. One of them says, "Hey, sweetheart," with a tone of voice that makes me think I'm in college again. I quickly shuffle to the kitchen and sign in. The kitchen supervisor, Ron, greets me with a huge grin and welcomes me with an apron. After I wash my hands, I begin chopping lettuce and strawberries. People start to line up long before lunch will be served at noon. They ask what's on the menu and make jokes with one of the regular workers, Chief. Ron tells me about his new puppy and how she stands on her hind legs and is already house-trained. While making small talk with the other volunteers, I smile at the clients as I hand them their food trays. Usually my gesture is met with a "Thank you, honey" or "Thanks, princess."

Other mornings, I head to the desk to help field all manner of requests:

"I need to put something in daytime storage."
"I need to sign up for a shower."
"I need to make a long-distance phone call."
"I need to check my mail."
"I need a cup of laundry detergent."
"I need to talk to a caseworker."

The needs encompass anything and everything required for getting by: diapers, dog food, winter coats, jobs, and bus passes. I'm overwhelmed by this lack. If there is an abundance of anything, it is urgency and stress.

One morning, I watch an older black woman holding a five-month-old baby in one arm and clasping the hand of a little girl with the other. The girl is the same age as my twins, maybe a little younger, maybe three or four. They're sitting in chairs, half falling asleep. The woman nudges the little girl and hands her the baby. The little girl scoots back in the chair to make room for the baby to sit between her legs, clutching him around the middle. They both stare quietly at the floor while the grandmother dozes off. I want so much to scoop up the baby in my arms and bounce him around. A few minutes later, they approach the desk, and I coo at the five-month-old with his big brown eyes and tufts of black hair, and compliment the little girl's winter hat bearing Minnie Mouse. She beams at me, twirling her two braids. I tell her she is a great big sister, and her grandmother agrees. The girl beams some more. I'm overcome, because I want to do something, but it's not my place. I wish I knew their story.

It has only been a month that I've served three times a week at the Shalom Community Center and at the Interfaith

Winter Shelter. Such a short time, yet I have seen and felt so much.

Each time I've gone, there's a moment when I seize up a little. Every single time. It happens when someone screams something obscene and it sounds like a fight is about break out, or when someone walks up in the lunch line and is clearly drunk or high and a little more than belligerent. It even happens when I notice the small things—the bad teeth, the matted hair, the mismatched and dirty clothes.

I think, Do I really want to do community with these people? I catch myself, with my feet pointed to the door and my hand on my jacket. Something in me wants to bolt and forget this whole thing, because these needs seem so unfamiliar to me—not just unknown but foreign. Not only do I not understand, but I don't see it clearly. I see their problems, yes. I recognize their issues and even potential "solutions" for their lives. I see what I've been conditioned to see, and this means I see people who are homeless and jobless. Maybe this translates to faithless, too—untrustworthy or lazy or weak. In other words, I see people I normally would ignore and avoid on a regular basis. I have trouble seeing beyond the borders of their clothing and the fringes of their unraveling shirts or Salvation Army and Goodwill sweatshirts.

So why am I here?

As the lunch shift closes up one day, a mother and a young boy, maybe seven or eight years old, come in at the last minute. We fill up two heaping plates of tamales, rice, and cheese, with extra fruit for them. I watch her try to figure out where to go. At nearby tables, a group of people lounge and digest their food, a coma setting in. The mother sets down her bags but looks uncertain. She tells the boy to use two hands to carry his plate, much in the same tone I use with my kids when they have a glass full of milk that's swishing around and threatening to spill. As I make a move to run around to the other side and help her, Heather, another woman I've often seen at the shelter, walks up to her and asks if she needs help and wants any more food. Heather adds that there's a family room in the back, where it's a little quieter, and she picks up the mother's things and leads her and the boy back to that area.

I watch this, thinking about all the ways it is difficult for me to cross over in so many scenarios. It's hard for me to enter into this space and community, even though I've served in soup kitchens and shelters in various places before. My faith feels oddly distant, and I keep having to call it to my mind. There's a disjointed reality here that isn't shiny and glitzy like in the movies about people who do something bold and surprising, and they have awesome self-revelations. Instead, I have to contend with my discomfort, my imperfections, and the grittiness of this place.

Why does this feel so significant? Why am I making it such a big deal? There's something more for me to see here, and it's just starting to shimmer on the surface.

For me to be in community with the people in front of me is a way of transgressing boundaries. These transgressions are at the heart of the blessedness of the promiscuous. It means taking in all of who these people are, just as I expect people to take in all of who I am—the good and the bad, the ideals and judgments, the hopes and flaws.

But, it's not just about me. I see how hard it is for these people around me to cross over toward me. And that may be not because it is hard for them but because of all the ways we (I mean I) put up blocks—mentally, socially, physically—that prevent anyone from crossing over and shattering all our presumptions and conditioning. Crossing over seems easier for those like Heather who automatically see and understand people's needs. I've watched her take care of people like this mother and her son in so many ways, but I know, like any of us, she's not perfect. That's not ultimately the point, though, right? Isn't this redeemed life about love and grace not in spite of but through our imperfections?

What keeps happening now in the continuous crossing over is an affirmation of not just the other's humanity but also my humanity. For now, this is why I keep showing up. I need to be regularly and blatantly impressed with the miracle of humanity all around me, to realize that the people in front of me are my people and not "those people." I'm choosing to show up—imperfectly, with all my judgmental thoughts that I have to squish down out of my brain. I show up to be reminded that my humanity is not dependent on what I wear or how I smell or what I think or see, but is rooted in the *imago Dei* as I experience it always in radical connection to those around me. I show up to cross over again and again to that reality always just beyond my peripheral vision, where the incarnate God is present even in the people and places I least expect, and least of all in me.

A queer spirituality is about both hospitality and solidarity. One is not found without the other, because once we truly make space for each other, we are bound up in one another. When embodied lives collide and intersect with each other, a kind of bedlam of disintegrating categories occurs. In the unadulterated beauty of that promiscuous intermingling, we discover the ways God is incarnate among us.

Notes

1. *Mean Girls*, directed by Mark Waters (Los Angeles, CA: Paramount Home Entertainment, 2004), widescreen special collector's edition DVD.

2. Patrick S. Cheng, *Radical Love: An Introduction to Queer Theology* (New York: Seabury, 2011), 1.

3. Kathleen T. Talvacchia, *Queering Christianities: Lived Religion in Transgressive Forms* (New York: New York University Press, 2015), 163.

4. José Esteban Muñoz, *Disidentifications: Queers of Color and the Performance of Politics* (Minneapolis: University of Minnesota Press, 1999), 25.

5. "6 Latinos Killed by US Cops This Week—and Media Ignored It," *TeleSUR*, July 9, 2016, https://tinyurl.com/y7ra4svc.

4

The Sacrament of Bodies

Your body is not a temple, it's an amusement park. Enjoy the ride.
—Anthony Bourdain, *Kitchen Confidential: Adventures in the Culinary Underbelly*

When I was ten or eleven, I started lifting weights.

I had a science teacher who had wiry, muscular arms—not large, but defined—and shoulders that looked like they could carry or handle anything. I admired them. She looked strong and exuded a quiet confidence and capability. I asked her about them once ("What did you do to get them?"), and she said she did twenty-five push-ups every day and lifted some weights. Somehow I convinced my parents to get two ten-pound weights, and I started using them daily, doing curls, shoulder presses, and butterfly presses while standing in front of a mirror in the living room.

Even though my parents didn't fight me on it, they often expressed their disapproval. "Your arms are going to look like a man's arms," my father would say to me. "Why do you want to look like a boy?" my mother would ask, exasperated.

For some reason, I was cognizant about muscles early on. Not only was I aware of them, I was drawn to them. Now, of course, I am obsessed with Michelle Obama's beautiful arms and the way she transformed my view of the First Lady by being unabashedly a woman of power and beauty. I have always liked the idea of looking and feeling strong.

From day one, I was a blur of activity—not unlike my six-year-old daughter, who is always bouncing, jumping, twirling, and climbing. As much as I was able, I would be out on my bike with the neighborhood kids and would return home covered in mud. I wanted to do anything and everything outside—to run on trails or in parks, chase after Frisbees, explore and wander off on my own. I would climb trees as high as I could until my mother found me and shrieked at me to climb back down. I wanted to feel it all—the sun and the wind, the cold and the rain, being outside where Mother Nature would wake me up. I loved the feeling of dirt from the mountains under my nails and on the soles of my feet.

Generally, though, my brother and I weren't encouraged to participate in athletics growing up. I'd always begged to play on the kids' soccer team and do more than the annual church volleyball tournament. I wanted to go to sports camps like my friends and to be on all the sports teams. But my parents always responded that studying was going to get me to college and that sports were not important.

The implicit message was that our bodies weren't meant

to be much more than containers for our brains, as if they were machines that needed only to be regularly maintained, groomed, and cleaned so as to be presentable. Yet our bodies are more than empty, inanimate vehicles for our consciousness. They mean something. They are constantly perceived and read, interpreted and shaped by external cultural forces. Many are violently forced to conform to that elusive and arbitrary standard eternalized by magazine covers.

In the Christianity in which I grew up, bodies were explained as a part of God's creation but not necessarily good. They were created by God's hands, but they were expected to be clothed and closeted. Anything that had to do with the body was always diminished because of the call to "live by the Spirit, I say, and do not gratify the desires of the flesh" (Galatians 5:16).

From the get-go, queerness undoes this dichotomy between mind and body, and the subsequent marginalization of bodies, by deliberately, purposefully centering bodies: how they move, how they breathe, how they express themselves, and how they experience pain and violence, lust and sex, desire and intimacy. More than that, queerness recognizes the temptation toward dichotomy and bridges these binaries, healing the gulf. It fills in the spaces we tend to leave empty and makes whole what is broken. A queer spirituality then invites us to see the possibility that our bodies are the sacramental—the holy, ordinary, sacred, and real-world—means in which we receive grace and salvation.

Bodies Matter

I first took sex education as a fourth-grader. None of it really made any sense to me, but I was fascinated with the anatomy portion of it: what genitalia look like on the inside and outside, with tubes and veins, muscles and sacs. I talked about it at home once, and my parents could barely hide their embarrassment.

Our brains, of course, try to impose order on chaos, so my parents did what made sense to them: they convinced themselves that this curiosity was a sign of blessing—I was meant to become a doctor, one of the ultimate dreams they had for me. So they forced themselves to deal with it because it was medicalized and objectified, sterilized and contained in scientific language, there were no real fluids to explain or mop up.

Of course, that's not real life. Bodies are messy and awkward in real life. Bodies are asymmetrical and not at all like the posters showing perfectly geometrical and anatomical representations of bodies. Bodies have secretions and fluids that crust over sometimes. Bodies get hungry and thirsty, and they need rest, touch, and sometimes moisturizing lotion. Well, lotion does help.

Even in the Bible, from day one, we read about bodies—bodies made out of dirt, bodies exposed, bodies covered up. There are a lot of naked bodies in the Old Testament, as well as in the Gospels, where bodies are prominent, with story after story of Jesus's healing encounters with the likes of Bartimaeus and Lazarus. Many people sought out Jesus simply to receive a miraculous touch or gesture on their bodies—bodies with sensory disabilities (blind and deaf), bodies with physical or mobility disabilities, bodies with chronic health conditions.

There's the story found in Mark 5 of the hemorrhaging woman who suffered for twelve years from an ailment that had no clear medical diagnosis according to the experts of that time—a woman whose condition worsened even after all the money, time, and hope poured into these futile assessments. Driven by desperation, she sought Jesus out. The gospel writers don't give us very much information about the life of the hemorrhaging woman, but we might assume she had to feel the daily onslaught of doctors poking and prodding her entire body, taking samples of her fluids, putting her whole life under the proverbial microscope, and then reducing her body to an object of mysterious horror and fascination. She experienced severe isolation because of the impurity of this persistent bleeding. According to Jewish tradition, she was unholy and unclean. And she knew it. She was deemed untouchable.

Only seen as an object of disease, this nameless woman was perpetually bleeding and visibly dying, without clear cause or explanation. Her condition involved a visceral pain that crossed every possible physical, spiritual, emotional boundary in her life, right through to her soul, yet it was imperceptible to those around her, even those intimately tied to her. I caught a glimpse of the depth of isolation and loneliness she must have felt when I found myself in a hospital bed, imprisoned by frail flesh struggling at the other end of numerous exploratory surgeries to understand the cause of my infertility. That hard, strange experience brought me closer to my humanity, and after working through anger, grief, and confusion, it brought me closer to the fragility of humanity—not only of my loved ones, but of all those around me.

I wonder about the other bodies in the life of this woman—her friends and family. Did she have parents who struggled with shame of their daughter, now an outcast? Did she have siblings who felt guilty for seeing her simply as dirty and who forgot what it was like to chase her, play with her, hug her, and hold her hand as they walked to school together? Did she have a husband or children? What was it like to not touch them or be touched by them for twelve years? What was it like to not have children running between her legs or entreating her to sit so they could dog-pile her for an hour for the sole purpose of being near her?

"If I but touch his clothes, I will be made well," she said to herself (Mark 5:28). She carefully made her way to Jesus and let her fingers brush the edge of his cloak. Then, the Scriptures tell us, "Immediately her hemorrhage stopped; and she felt in her body that she was healed of her disease" (verse 29). I can only imagine what it was like for her to get her life and body back—to finally feel the butterfly kisses of her children and the embrace of her husband and parents.

The healing was thorough and complete. It not only gave her body back to her but also gave her body back to other bodies. She was made whole for herself and for the sake of the community. Her body was the site for salvation.

Jesus's body matters, too. Power had gone out of him (verse 30); something shifted or changed in his body. He turned around, looking at the sea of faces and bodies pressed in on him, looking for the source of this change, and asked, "Who touched my clothes? Who touched me?" Of course, the disciples were bewildered by this, as they looked around and saw people reaching out to him from every direction. But Jesus knew, in his body, that someone had touched him in a particular way, enough that it made him stumble a little. He paused, stood still, and tried to understand what had affected him in this way. The woman came forward in shock, fearful, and fell down before him. Instead of reprimanding her, he extolled her and sent her on her way.

Jesus went on his way, too, his body changed from the inside out.

Our bodies and what happens to them are intricately connected to our worldview. When he was twelve or thirteen years old, my father woke up one morning and was paralyzed. He wasn't able to get up, move, or walk, and he simply lay in bed for a year. His parents tried one thing after another and finally found an acupuncturist who cured him. There was little explanation for his healing, but my father talks about it as a moment that changed his understanding of his body, to see the temporality of it. And in response to his season of paralysis, he cultivated this awareness and a surprising gratitude.

Being flesh and blood matters. The experiences our bodies go through, large and small—both the trauma and the daily nudges and collisions from the external world—are mapped out on our bodies. All of this makes us.

Bodies matter so much that Jesus came back from death in his own body, in that same despised, abused, and tortured body. It's an incredible picture of solidarity, not an embrace of violence. It is a reminder that the exclusion, diminishment, and dehumanization of bodies are still realities in the world and that Jesus Christ, Emmanuel, that is "God-with-Us" means way more than empathy. That "the Word became flesh and lived among us" (John 1:14) means the incarnation is a shared, lived experience. The embodied, wounded, and scarred Jesus shapes our understanding of how and why our bodies matter.

Queerness is restoration. A queer spirituality is queer when we who are diverted from our path to wholeness find healing in our bodies.

Queer Bodies

Queerness begins from the premise that bodies matter. We need our bodies. More than that, we *are* our bodies. We are our muscles and joints, our bones and marrow, our aches and pain. Queerness doesn't judge, contain, or see our bodies as things to be conquered or mastered, whether by language or label. Concerning bodies today, queerness does disrupt and undo convention, tradition, and all those scripts that say a body should be or do or look like one thing. Queerness sometimes remakes bodies. It then transforms the space in which these bodies move, live, and breathe, so that queer bodies allow for multiple ways of being and connecting by revealing new experiences of the *imago Dei*, the image of God.

To capture the *imago Dei*, whether through painting, scribbling, sculpture, photography, or iconography, is a timeless human endeavor. I loved watching the development of our children's portrayals of the human body. Their early efforts involved drawing a large circle, inserting eyes and a mouth, and adding lines sticking out of the circle to signify arms and legs. Connected to these lines, they added various ovals with claws at the end of each for hands and feet. Then they included specific genitalia. All of it was so fascinating—this process of depicting and making sense of bodies.

Photographer Robert Mapplethorpe, considered by art historians to be one of the most significant artists of the twentieth century, exhibited his work at the renowned Kinsey Institute in Bloomington, Indiana. A few years back, when I was auditing a gender studies course held in the building right across from the Kinsey, I was able to see a few of his works firsthand. Most of them are nude bodies in a variety of shades, all photographed in black and white. These arresting photographs capture a consummate beauty that is both formal and raw.

Mapplethorpe was particularly known for his 1986 solo exhibition *Black Males* and the subsequent *The Black Book,* a controversial work for its nude, erotic depictions of black men that were widely criticized for being exploitative. The photographs were largely phallocentric and sculptural, focusing on segments of the subject's bodies—for example, showing only an upper thigh or looking through the legs to the face. Much of the work that engaged these photographs understandably criticized their objectification of the black male body, both for displaying the men as passive, decorative objects (a treatment more often reserved for female subjects) and for perpetuating the hypersexuality of black male identity We might interpret Mapplethorpe's perspective in these photos as admiration—lifting up the black male body as glorious and sublime—but his sexual and racial identity (gay and white) complicates this perspective. The black male bodies were not photographed in a vacuum but by someone with privilege and power, and these dynamics remind us that not only does representation matter but so does the identity of the one behind the camera.

This example illustrates that our bodies are often defined in terms of race, gender, sexuality, and ability, and these definitions matter. It means something when we talk about bodies—how we see them, how we present them, how they are represented, how we interact with them. And it matters what relationships are present. Nothing is ever simply one thing. Nothing is ever completely straightforward. If we look below the surface, we might see countless points of overlap. Our bodies are messy and complicated, and because of these complications, our bodies, especially queer bodies, are often recipients of the cruel brutality of systems and structures that need certain bodies to be marginalized and viewed as the Other. To shove, push and pull, or force bodies into these categories is not just linguistic coercion. It is emotional, spiritual, and often acted out physically, with sexual assault and rape being one example. Some bodies have to establish their own reality and agency, and they do so by asserting their bodies over and against other bodies.

To make space for a queer spirituality, then, is to challenge these systems of power that rely on the visible, verbal, and violent constructions of bodies. Queer bodies embody lived forms of experience that resist these structures. They are themselves redemptive, and not only in the religious sense. We might think of religion as only a conglomeration of sacred texts maintained by trained elites and experienced in houses of worship—a system of beliefs and practices. But for many queer religious people, "their bodily and their spiritual experience are the twin lodestars of their lives."[1] In fact, the embodied faith of queerness might give us a wider space for creativity and complexity in all the intersections of lived experience. The ordinary and everyday experiences of bodies are where we encounter those deepest connections that give us an expansive view of the universe, of the divine, of eternity, of God's kingdom come.

Christianity is a location of the most revolutionary kind of queerness. From the beginning, we are told, "You have a body," and many institutions have tried to tell us how to manage it. But it is and was never meant to be a normalizing system, one that contains and neatly compartmentalizes reality, because Christianity is all about the body. Every sect, every strain and lineage of Christianity is centered on the body—the body at Calvary, the body of Christ, the suffering body, the glorified body. All of Christianity is anchored in the body and a queer understanding of the way bodies are meant to relate to one another.

Queer bodies desire sight and desire to be seen. Queer bodies desire belonging and connection, as when Bartimaeus on the side of the road received sight and the hemorrhaging woman received life and community.

Sacrament of Bodies

Certainly, our bodies are made for pleasure, whether it is the enjoyment of food or sex or recreation or relaxation, but pleasure is always connected to the experience of making whole, and this is always in our bodies. Understanding bodies as sacrament helps me live this more fully. Our bodies are sites for healing, for meaning making, for transformation—in other words, for salvation.

But what exactly are sacraments? Are they simply rituals that are set apart and infused with something magical? Whenever I have a question, I go to my *BOO*. I don't mean Andy, my husband of fourteen years, but the *Book of Order* and, specifically, the Presbyterian Church (USA) Directory of Worship,[2] which describes sacraments in this way: "The Reformed tradition understands Baptism and the Lord's Supper to be Sacraments, instituted by God and commended by Christ. Sacraments are signs of the real presence and power of Christ in the Church, symbols of God's action. Through the

Sacraments, God seals believers in redemption, renews their identity as the people of God, and marks them for service."

Sacraments are signs of the real presence and power of Christ in the church. They are the visible, genuine rendering of God's grace to God's hungry and thirsty people. Whenever the sacraments are celebrated in worship, the objects, movements, and words—all that is lifted up in that sacramental moment—are meaningful, because they are instituted by God and commended by Christ. In other words, they matter because of the presence of God's Holy Spirit through the people present, our connection to the traditions and histories of the universal church, and our trust in the power of the meaningful words to accompany the sacraments. They do work on our bodies.

The early church, following Jesus, took three primary material elements of life—water, bread, and wine—to become basic symbols of God's abundant, lavish offering of life to us as Jesus had offered his life. They are physical and embodied. Being washed with the water of baptism, Christians receive new life in Christ and present their bodies to be living sacrifices to God. Eating bread and drinking wine, we receive the sustaining presence of Christ, remember God's covenant promise, and reciprocate that covenant by committing ourselves to the body of Christ.

Sacraments are the holy enacted in the stuff of everyday life: kids, school, grandparents, church, the grocery store, our gardens, playgrounds, coffee places, pubs, Band-Aids on boo-boos, and butterfly kisses.

What exactly do sacraments do? How do they do what they do? What does this mean in the context of bodies? Many of us often forget the activity of the Holy Spirit in sacraments. Perhaps, we are weirded out by the Holy Spirit, unruly and untamable. If we neglect the activity of the Spirit who seals these promises of life and love onto our lives over and over, then we miss out on the continuous gracious work and transformation happening to us not only as individuals but also as a community. In this way, sacraments are an embodied invitation to God's story of redemption.

The Orthodox tradition offers us some lovely ways to think about sacrament and liturgy that are very different from what I grew up in, yet they resonate so deeply. Liturgy is not simply words in the bulletin that are read aloud but a collective and corporate expression of God's story of redemption. So the whole church itself embodies the liturgy and sacrament—proclaiming and witnessing at every moment, Sunday to Saturday, to the work of God and God's kingdom. The Eucharist takes us beyond the table. We focus so much on what happens in the pews and the pulpit, the bread and the cup that we overlook the process our bodies take toward the table and then the journey outward from the table.

This way of thinking about sacrament also takes us beyond all the traditional images of church—font, pulpit, pews, stained-glass windows. The work and process are thoroughly integrated with the whole person, from morning to evening, as soon as one's feet touch the ground upon getting out of bed. Thus, wherever a person sets foot, it is a part of the journey toward, and away from, and then eventually back toward the table again, to the place of Communion—of reconciliation, parity, integration, and radical belonging—to the kind of existence where all of these are embodied realities.

So the liturgy shows us, in the Eucharist and in baptism, a thin place, a moment where the veil between heaven and earth becomes transparent and we see in a mirror, a little less darkly, a shimmering image of God's kingdom come. We see a glimpse of that being and becoming fuller, more alive, more beloved. But that process of being and becoming is always about our bodies.

It's the sacrament of body and bodies that does work in our lives. Why else would Jesus tell his disciples that they would eat of his flesh and drink his blood to find eternal life? This scandalizing, risqué fetishizing of Jesus's body and blood through the experience of the Eucharist is a kind of othering, a holy othering. We imagine and fantasize that we are consuming the body of Jesus, the Son of God, the Son of Man, fully divine and human, and as we take his body and blood in our own bodies, we are undone and remade. It is a consensual act—the invitation to the table and our acceptance and submission to it—and then it becomes a moment of "consensual salvation."[3]

A queer spirituality entreats us to see that salvation has to do with our bodies, and that salvation isn't about a golden ticket to heaven but about the here and now—our experience in and through our materiality in this moment. Every moment becomes sacramental (holy, set apart, and a space for the Holy Spirit to play), and what seems quotidian becomes a supplication for what is divinely felt: a taste, a sip, a sprinkle of that profound connection.

My modus operandi as a mother is to make my children run and play, so that they can feel and be in their bodies as much as possible. I support a wide variety of physical activity: soccer, free play on playgrounds, long walks and hikes, swimming, throwing a football or hitting a Wiffle ball, and whatever other games they make up. In fact, I demand it. Every day, I force them to ride their bikes, although it's easiest to convince the youngest, Ozzie. Yes, all three of them, the four-year-old and the six-year-olds, ride pedal bikes already, and it's absolutely terrifying. Ozzie doesn't seem to have any inhibitions; he fearlessly and maniacally laughs every time he goes downhill, zipping by us as he barely dodges parked cars and mailboxes. I didn't learn to ride a bike until I was maybe eight or nine, when I had a clear sense of the rules of gravity and inevitability of pain. Still, in the words of the writer of Hebrews, who asks us to "consider how to provoke one another to love and good deeds" (Hebrews 10:25), I spur them to be active with their bodies as much as possible. I do that because ultimately I know they will sleep easily and without a fight at a decent hour, which means I might have a chance at sleep, too.

Bodies move, but they also need to be still. And these days, mine seems to need more and more of that blessed rest. Certainly, my body doesn't jump out of bed, raring to go, as Ozzie does. In the way he hits the ground running as soon as he pops up, he resembles a Whac-A-Mole, except that I can't shove him back into the hole to make him sleep ten more minutes. When I force myself to wake up, I can feel every joint now stiff with daily aging. Muscles in my neck are aching from the strange angles I lie in to accommodate Ozzie when he sneaks into bed in the middle of the night, throwing his body perpendicular to mine, with his feet kicking me in the head or back. When I place my feet on the floor, I gingerly step down the hallway until my toes wake up, and I clutch the wall as Ozzie zips past me or through my legs in this perpetual race with me. There's a kind of messiness in my feelings about the kids' movement and stillness. How I love to see those moving, jumping, and dancing bodies, but how I adore their sleeping bodies, too—their quiet, temporarily inert bodies.

I watch them sleep, and sometimes I feel consumed with worry and uncertainty. I love their bodies. Every chance I get, I chase them and gather them up in my arms, nuzzle their necks, and smell their hairline, where remnants of their baby hair still sprout. I squeeze them, I cover them with kisses, I nibble on their toes and earlobes. I want them to know and feel pleasure in their bodies, but most of all, I want them to know their bodies are loved, and how to love their bodies themselves.

Despite all that, I'm still learning to love my own body—my flesh, my skin, my muscles, my fat rolls, my flopping arms, my sausage fingers, and my moon face. As a teenager, I found that my body was subject to constant scrutiny, to judgment and criticism. It happened when I gained fifteen pounds after my senior year in high school. It happened when I was in middle school and out in the bright, full sun every day in the summers, which sprinkled freckles all across my nose, to my parents' disdain. It happened on a campout with a group of high school friends, who asked if my pubic hair was straight like my Asian hair (which wasn't naturally straight, actually), or was it curly like theirs?

What I've slowly come to realize over the years is that it's difficult to embrace other bodies fully and genuinely if we do not receive our own bodies first. It's the Golden Rule, after all: love your neighbor as yourself. Bodies are more than containers for our souls. They are themselves so deeply spiritual that God thought it was necessary to have one, too.

Queerness recognizes that we are embodied. It is about the bone and marrow, messy discharges and fluids. To live into a queer spirituality is to desire and love the body in a sacramental way. The sacraments are messy, too, even though we try to contain them in pewter and sanded-down fonts. Thankfully, though, we're not called to be perfect. We're called to love. We're called to love bodies and to love from our bodies.

Notes

1. Kathleen T. Talvacchia, Mark Larrimore, and Michael F. Pettinger, eds., *Queer Christianities: Lived Religion in Transgressive Forms* (New York: New York University Press, 2015), 7.

2. The Book of Worship of the Presbyterian Church (USA) is a resource that guides and shapes the worship services of the local church, and more.

3. Marcella Althaus-Reid, *Indecent Theology: Theological Perversions in Sex, Gender and Politics* (London: Routledge, 2000), 154.

5

Being Undone

Let's face it. We're undone by each other. And if we're not,
we're missing something.

—Judith Butler, *Undoing Gender*

I was home from college one weekend shortly after my parents moved back to Colorado. After dinner, we slowly
cleaned up. I paused for a moment and sat down in the living
room. Suddenly, my mother and father began quarreling, the
way they used to fight when I was a little girl. This time,
however, I wasn't afraid, and I didn't hide under the covers, whispering desperate prayers over and over. "Please God,
don't let them get a divorce," I'd pray, because to my eight-
year-old mind, divorce seemed like the end of the world.

Although I wasn't afraid this time, I held my breath, frozen,
because I hadn't seen a fight like this in a while. They were
both in the kitchen, but I could see them from the couch. My
mother was gesticulating with a spoon in one hand, shriek-
ing about the long hours of thankless work with him for the

church. My father stood up and began bellowing back, trying to get a word in edgewise. Then, as though in slow motion, I saw her turn and reach for the small plant in a terra cotta pot on the counter behind her, and in one smooth motion, she chucked it at him.

I remembered seeing that green plant in the apartment they had occupied in Princeton when my father decided to go to seminary. I was amazed it had survived the trip after graduation back to Colorado with them. I wondered why they brought it, since it was the kind of plant you could just buy at the local grocery store.

I dove in between them and swatted it to the floor before it hit anyone. I looked at the dirt on the carpet, scattered on top of the broken pieces of the pot, with the leaves of the plant crushed and strewn at my feet. Something in me snapped. I squeezed my fists and screamed, "Stop it! Just stop it! Stop fighting!" as if all the years of pent-up angst from hearing them scream at each other were bursting forth like water over a breaking dam. "Why are you still fighting like this?! Just get a divorce if you hate each other so much!"

They barely looked at me and simply circled each other like two predators in the wild trying to protect their territory. My mother went to her room and locked the door, but as usual, I could hear her talking angrily. After any fight, she used to talk to no one in particular—maybe to the dishes while cleaning up the kitchen or to the walls of her closet as she folded the laundry. My father left the apartment. I cleaned up the remains of the houseplant and tossed the mess into the garbage.

My first perspective on marriage was molded on my parents' marriage, which was a relationship that often struck me as deeply lacking. I never saw them express physical affection, and it seemed as if the volume and tone of their voices were constantly at a fever pitch, intense and combative. Certainly, they had stressful times as much as anyone else, especially as immigrants trying to negotiate survival in this country. Still, I held up their life together next to rom-coms and Disney princess movies, and judged it according to some imaginary happily-ever-after that I assumed must exist after the credits finished rolling.

It wasn't until after my honeymoon, when I moved into the church manse with Andy, that I realized marriage was all quite a bit more involved than flying off on a magic carpet toward the horizon, where some easy, perfect union awaited. Nearly every day of our lives was filled with the strenuous task of simply living together in the same space—trying to do the simple work of adjustment and compromise even as our sense of selves was constantly colliding around what missionary and evangelical author Elisabeth Elliot described as the four areas of marital conflict: "bedroom, bathroom, breakfast, and budget."[1]

The traditional scripts around marriage came undone for me many years later, as I saw that the formulas for a sound marriage were untenable—not just for me, but for so many around us—because there was little room for choice or agency. As Andy and I watched a large percentage of our friends' marriages end in separation and divorce, I realized that marriage was just something everyone did, falling into it like herds of lemmings into an ocean of some idea of adulthood. But viewed at the level of different societies, the whole concept of marriage, like ideas around identity, relationships, desire, and community, is complex. Some people are not able to marry, and others are able to marry and have many wives. Some spouses are happy in marriages arranged by others or resign themselves to marriages that hide their true desires and lifestyles. At worst, marriages can be coercive and abusive, oppressive and violent. Marriage also has economic implications: it is entrenched in systems that control wealth, inheritance, and prosperity. And religion plays a role, as when Christian symbols, rituals, and stories around marriage are used to prop up one kind of relationship, one kind of intimacy and sexuality. In real life, then, marriage isn't just about individuals finding that one true love or that happy ending.

In the Name of Love

Truth be told, love—actual real-life-blood-sweat-and-tears love—is weird. And everything that Hollywood presents as a love story compounds the confusion. For example, there's all the nonsense about soul mates and destiny and waiting for "the one." Although I gave up those notions before meeting Andy, even now, as I write about and ponder marriage, I catch myself spinning my wedding ring on my finger. Deep down inside, I wonder whether we are all following some script simply for the proliferation of the species and civilization.

I know I was compatible with other boys before Andy—maybe in some ways even more compatible. Yes, definitely, I had more in common with some of them, like enjoying sci-fi movies or enjoying the outdoors. It's easy to say that in the end, something was missing from each relationship. But what was it? Did I ultimately need my parents' approval? Was it maturity? Readiness? Timing?

Even still, the timing wasn't perfect with Andy. We were finishing up seminary, and he was ready to take a call to pastor his first church. I was still in school with one more year, and my ordination exams loomed around the corner. That first year of marriage, we lived together only on the weekends, which was hellish. It felt like we had to cram in all the catching up, flirting, fighting, and being together in two days. The perfect storm of stress from marriage and school, marriage and work schedules, and marriage and two different life seasons battered our little vessel in the beginning. Then there was the commute. East Coast commutes with all the confusing turnpikes and bridges, tolls and unexpected delays can really wreak havoc on your sanity.

Early on, I began to ask myself whether I had made the right decision. Our marriage didn't look anything like true love in the movies or love songs or those snippets I could remember from Shakespeare. "Falling in love" became a fiercely significant question. How exactly did it matter? Those marriage vows felt heavy. I tried to reconcile my feelings with the ideals. But all the perspectives on "traditional" marriage have created a war zone where all sorts of party lines are drawn in its changing sands. Suddenly, I couldn't wrap my mind around marriage and what it meant in the midst of all these questions. Furthermore, it was not only a question of decision but one of choice: Had I made the right choice? It was unsettling, and statistics on divorce didn't help, though they made more sense.

The vows and shiny rings made it feel as if love was all that mattered and was necessary. Then the bills started to come in. Work schedules had to be negotiated on a regular basis. The tube of toothpaste was constantly missing its cap (usually my fault). The creamer was left out on the counter (again, my fault). And the dirty clothes were piling up in the laundry room (Andy's fault—too many socks and undershirts). I began to look around and wonder, *Where's the love now?*

Quite simply, falling in love just wasn't enough. Here's the thing. Contrary to assumptions about one of the largest modern-day institutions, marriage wasn't actually always about love. In previous eras, romantic love was a laughable, even despised reason for marriage, and definitely the least practical.

Up until the eighteenth century in the West, most young people would not choose their own spouses on the basis of something like love, because notions of happiness and fulfillment weren't a part of the equation for maintaining social order. But this began to shift when the spread of wage labor allowed young people to be self-sufficient, so they wouldn't have to rely on their families for an inheritance or dowry. Likewise, nineteenth-century Enlightenment ideas and the age of revolution across Europe emphasized individual rights like the pursuit of happiness, including ideas like marrying for love. Yet these movements caused massive upheaval, and as societies scrambled to reassert more patriarchal structures, narratives emerged around the difference between men's and women's roles. Men belonged in the public sphere as the breadwinners, while women, whose constitutions were presumed to be delicate and moral, belonged in the private sphere at home as angelic bearers of domesticity.

Early in the twentieth century, especially in the United States, we see a Golden Age of Marriage, with huge numbers of people living out this ideal of different but shared responsibilities. It wasn't until the latter half of the century that we see the pendulum swing back. Issues of economic and social inequalities rooted in gender, race, and class now reveal the inadequacy of the male-as-breadwinner model.

My parents have been married for forty years now. They will never divorce. In the heat of a moment, they might threaten it, as if saying the words out loud was a way of trying it out, to hear and feel that possibility, that unknown void. In fact, for them, that separation, that individuation and self-sufficiency, would be too much to bear alone. They do nearly everything together. Only when my mother is tired from an early morning will she stay home while my father goes to church meetings, but it rarely happens. I used to wonder if codependency was present in their marriage, but I now see it as a companionship, a partnership. They rely on each other. I don't think they would credit some idealistic notion of love, not even the more evangelical perspective on "biblical marriage." But they do have a strong, abiding sense of duty, of God's covenant and faithfulness.

When more conservative Christians invoke "biblical marriage," they are referring to the Golden Age of Marriage as the ideal. In their minds, they're citing Adam and Eve, and maybe the passage in one of Paul's letters on wives submitting to their husbands, and maybe the intention of procreation. Yet there's no clear definition of "biblical marriage." There's Abraham and Sarah . . . and Hagar. There's Jacob and his situation with Leah and Rachel . . . and Bilhah . . . and Zilpah—basically, an arrangement that would appear scandalous today, somewhere in the same vein as *The Bachelor*. Then there's Solomon, with his hundreds of wives. At the other extreme, Jesus and, for that matter, Paul appear to have never settled down with anyone. Paul, who has that whole chapter in 1 Corinthians on marriage, seems to go back and forth on whether people should be married or not, based on the individual's capacity to control his or her passions. In sum, there is hardly a clear standard of "biblical marriage," yet that phrase is ubiquitous in our discussions about marriage today. The irony is that "biblical marriage" is really twentieth-century norms that are rooted in some notion of the nuclear family and homophobia.

Truthfully, I can't think of a time when I *didn't* think I would get married, have kids, have a career, and eventually

. . . something. It kind of goes black after that. Every happily-ever-after scenario I saw was love, then marriage, then a baby in a carriage. Our culture is so saturated with this one narrow view of marriage that I never questioned whether this would be my fate. It was so inherent that I didn't see the script until much later. And then I thought, "Good grief! Have we all been drinking the Kool-Aid with little thought about what everything actually means?"

I love and value my husband, our life together, and our family. But our arrangement is not for everyone, and it isn't fair to expect or require it of everyone. Even more, it's not right to grant some people privileges and benefits based on it. Because, let's be honest, no matter how hard we try, marriage—whether biblical or Christian or secular or civil, especially the way it is structured today in Western civilization—seems like it is hardly about love.

Conscious Coupling

I am writing this chapter near the fiftieth anniversary of *Loving v. Virginia*, the Supreme Court decision that overturned laws banning interracial marriage. In 1958, Richard Loving married Mildred Jeter in Washington, DC. He was white, and she was black and Native. Six weeks later, a sheriff arrived at their home with a warrant and dragged the couple out of bed. The Lovings spent five days in jail and were convicted of violating Virginia's ban on interracial marriages. But the Supreme Court ruled in 1967 that the freedom to marry was an essential personal right that could not be infringed by the state, and the Lovings were able to remain married in Virginia.

In 2003, when Andy and I decided to get married, I wasn't cognizant of the privilege we were afforded. After making our announcement and getting down to the nitty-gritty of all the wedding details, we reflected on how easy it was to walk over to the courthouse with friends who would stand as our witnesses, sign for a marriage license, and then simply *be* married by the proclamation of a few words and the provision of another signature. Neither of us was even a legal resident of New Jersey, where we were living as seminary students. It was easy to fall in love and then fall in line.

I remember the announcement of actress Gwyneth Paltrow and Coldplay frontman Chris Martin that they were separating after ten years of marriage. They called their separation "conscious uncoupling." Though I, like so many others, laughed at their words at the time, I keep thinking about the ways we talk about this strange and sacred union of people. The scripts around the institution of marriage do not make space for the words *choice* and *consent*, especially when it seems like everyone is forced to enter the same chute in order to get spit out as one particular kind of citizen. And then there are some who don't even get to make a choice at all.

In many ways, historically marriage was the legal avenue to reproduction for citizens, and it also affected the citizenship roles of men and women. In 1855, Congress declared that a woman of any origin or nationality became a citizen of the United States upon marrying an American man, so long as she met naturalization requirements (she had to be a "free white person").[2] The same law specified that the child of an American male citizen, born on US soil or abroad, was a US citizen. Both of these privileges were specific to gender; they were centered around the male.

Family and domestic life, once private, became fodder for state legislation. The state entered into this seemingly invincible relationship and shaped gender by enshrouding it in benefits for only one specific (read: heterosexual) kind of relationship, perpetuating the exclusion of many commitments and, necessarily, making women second-class citizens. There is a gender order wherein the male is privileged and the female is subordinate, and the female is useful only insofar she is coupled in a productive way with a male. Marriage, as sanctioned by the state, maintains this kind of relationship, and then that relationship perpetuates the gender order.

Furthermore, capitalism became a vehicle in which monogamy, and therefore the binding contract of marriage, was used to maintain the existence of civilized and advancing societies. Labor and economics are powerful forces that shape societies, and privatizing marriage was a necessity in order to continue to protect this institution and therefore this kind of society. Protecting marriage meant elevating marriage to a fantasy land of romance, true and eternal love, between a knight in shining armor and a damsel in distress, whose property and name would soon belong to the knight.

Establishing one's legitimacy is embedded even in the

mundane. When I decided to change my name to its current hyphenated form, I saw how easy it was to do so. I filled out a one-page application and turned it in to the local office of the Social Security Administration. A few weeks later, I received my new Social Security card. My last name echoed Andy's name and family. But, there's more, as the act of taking another last name has roots in the history of slavery and violent practices related to naming slaves and erasing whole lineages. The only thing kept alive was the idea of male ownership and identity, and present day cultural practices in the United States only solidify these structures. For a marrying woman, it was easy to obtain a new last name—a marker of maleness, whiteness, and privilege and of legitimacy. In contrast, Andy found that the process for him to change his last name would be much more involved, time-consuming, and in the end, not worth it. So he didn't do it. At the time, it never crossed my mind that this difference seemed odd.

Despite all the work done to pursue equal rights for women, seemingly inconsequential practices like this remain as vestiges of the past. Our society's benefits and privileges are male oriented and male dominated (and specifically, heteromale dominated). How much do we actually get to choose in this conscious coupling when the choices are limited and when consent means that your decision has to follow one track if you want the same benefits and privileges as those in the status quo? We have come a distance from *Loving v. Virginia* to legalizing same-sex marriage in the United States, but what we make normative doesn't necessarily erase continuous inequities in the larger consciousness of our society.

Queering Intimacy

In one of my favorite episodes of *Parks and Recreation*, the television show set in fictional small-town Pawnee, Indiana, department director Leslie Knope holds a marriage for two recently acquired penguins to help promote the Pawnee Zoo. Immediately after the marriage, the two penguins begin having sex in front of a crowd of children, who are informed by an adult in the audience that both penguins are actually males. This creates a bit of a stir in the town. The Bulge, a gay bar in Pawnee, later sends Leslie a wedding cake with two penguins on top to thank her for supporting the gay community. But she gets flak from the wider public for appearing to make a political statement, and on a local TV show, numerous callers ask her to resign. Fed up, Leslie adamantly insists she will not resign, nor will she annul the penguin wedding. The episode ends with Leslie driving the penguins from the Pawnee Zoo to a zoo in Iowa, where same-sex marriage is legal.

It's a hilarious, adorable story, but one that is actually realistic. Gay penguins are known to steal eggs from straight couples in an effort to become fathers. In other cases, a female may even temporarily associate with a male-male pair, mate with them, and leave her eggs with them. One German zoo provoked outrage from gay lobby groups after attempting to mate a group of gay male penguins with Swedish female birds who had been flown in especially to seduce them. The project was abandoned after the males refused to be "turned," showing no interest in their would-be mates. In 2002, a couple of penguins at a New York zoo who had been together for eight years were outed when keepers noticed that they were both males.

Many who categorize same-sex intimacies as immoral and illegal cite nature as well as offer biblical explanations. But along with these penguin stories, animals in the wild provide numerous examples to the contrary. In response to a transphobic comment on Facebook, biology teacher Grace Pokela posted a comment giving examples of deviations that *naturally* occur among numerous species in response to environmental conditions, individual and population size, and even loss of limbs. For example, Pokela tells of female flatworms that are females because "they lost a sword fight." Without a fully functioning penis, they transfer sperm through a process called penis fencing. Pokela concludes, "Don't use science to justify your bigotry. The world is way too weird for that shit."[3]

Queerness embraces and cultivates that weirdness. It sees deviation as normal and normative. It sees what is perplexing, rare, or unfamiliar as a possibility for a new, glorious iteration not only of humanity but of all creation. So then, queering marriage is not just about queering an institution or expectation, a social script, but about queering intimacy, queering connection, and ultimately again, queering identity and desire. Queering love, then, is widening the bounds around the possibility of that expression of love. And a queer spirituality is about reproducing that love as much as possible.

I write this during Pride Month, a time rooted in protest going back to the riots at Stonewall. There is much to lament as LGBTQIA people are targeted for violence, even murder, around the world, and discrimination is as commonplace and personal as the nearest public restroom. That history is still so close to us, yet, there is much that inspires hope. Yet there is much that inspires hope. Notably, in June 2015, the Supreme Court ruled in *Obergefell v. Hodges* that state-level bans on same-sex marriage are unconstitutional, a decision that had the effect of legalizing same-sex marriage in all states. Every year, the festivals, rallies, and street parties held around the country lift up the resilience and goodness of LGBTQIA communities. Most of all, Pridefest reminds us that love persists, and both beauty and joy are powerful tools for this daily resistance.

For a long time, marriage was seen as a natural building block for civilizations—but only applied to a particular kind of marriage based on economics, race, and gender. This changed when people decided to take hold of their destinies, follow the call of their hearts, and believe in the power of their choices. It revolutionized how we understand not just an individual person but the beauty of conscious and courageous coupling.

In other words, marriage isn't the be-all and end-all. But love is. Love, actually, is everything. As composer, actor, and playwright Lin-Manuel Miranda said, "Love is love is love is love is love."

After asking whether marriage is a way to make each person simply a cog in the machine—the state-regulated, capitalistic, heteropatriarchal structure that centers around property and material wealth—a queer spirituality shows us a more excellent way, to use the apostle Paul's words from the famous love chapter of 1 Corinthians 13. I'm still in the process of living into queerness, something I would not have been able to do without the love, support, and honest engagement of my spouse, Andy. When I first began to hint at my own shift toward queerness in casual ways, and then in marital counseling together, Andy's initial response was understandably fear and uncertainty. But he never elevated his worry about what it meant for our marriage above his love and concern for me.

We have gone through numerous changes throughout our marriage. Not just seasons of vocation or location, but we ourselves have changed, and we've learned to recalibrate our life together. Most days, it's not pretty, and it's far from ideal. There are days I'm ready to give up. I'm sure he has felt the same. Though it hasn't been easy, it has compelled us to reimagine covenant, faithfulness, and life together—to see that it isn't about possession or ownership, though everything in the scripts around marriage would make us look at each other as property.

As we continue to work through what it means that I identify as queer and how to reorient our lives toward each other, it has deepened my experience of love—love for Andy and love for our life together. I have become more fully myself, and then the most radical and revolutionary thing: I can be loved as myself, even if that self is drastically different from the person Andy married nearly fourteen years ago. But there is a glimmering of transformation in the midst of that intimate acceptance. Receiving it and giving it are enough for another week, another year, another lifetime.

I look at my parents now and notice the way they sit together on the couch, my father with an absentminded look on his face but tenderly stroking my mom's leg or knee as he listens to me chatter about my day. It's a surprising kind of physical affection that must have built up in these years since my brother and I left home to start our own adult lives. I see the way they, too, have changed.

People say we become our parents. I see it now in the way I say something in a certain way or feel my body in a particular posture or doing a gesture, and in my mind's eye, I see my mother and her mother saying or doing it, too, mimicking me. It happens with the way I stand or sit with my shoulders hunched or put on my makeup with my face against the mirror or chase Ellis, our boxer dog, out of the house, just as my maternal grandmother did. The tone of my voice or inflection in a certain phrase, most likely and usually about food; the edge to a screech when I'm losing it with the kids; and the quiet calm that overtakes me in a moment of chaos resemble my paternal grandmother. And I'm like my mother in the manic way I tackle certain projects—obsessive and focused.

Sometimes when I look at my hands, I now see the hands

my mother has in old photographs, like the one of the birth of my younger brother. She is sitting in the delivery bed, clutching him swaddled in a faded blue blanket as I sit nearby, a two-year-old buzzing with barely contained excitement. Whenever I look at this picture, my eyes aren't drawn to my bedhead pigtails or bright-red OshKosh B'Gosh overalls. I stare at her hands because it shocks me to see how familiar they look. They're . . . my hands. So now I notice her hands all the time. I remember looking at them once when Ozzie, our third, was born. I observed then how much they've changed with the years yet still somehow maintain such strength and tenderness simultaneously.

And when I fight, I use my hands as my mother does. I throw, I wring, I squeeze, I clench, and I pound the table as she does. However, Andy is not my father, and when he fights, he knows how to coax me out of my cave. In this way, I fight like my father, too, because, like him, I withdraw and want to escape. I'm not just my mother, I realize, and I haven't fallen far from either tree. There's a whole forest of my ancestors within me, a root system of a large, ancient organism connecting all of us—all their dreams, their seasons, their fights.

"This is a season," an older married friend reminded me when the twins (now six and in first grade) were first born and we were running on lonely fumes with no sleep and no sex. But it's a season that rings familiar not because I've experienced it before. I feel it in my bones. I feel it in my cells, in my blood, and on my skin.

Recent research suggests we inherit the trauma of our ancestors. This rings true for me. Maybe these are the ghosts of my father's and mother's religion. No doubt, I've acquired remnants of all their genetic blueprints—their quirks and idiosyncrasies, but also their struggles, their scripts, their fears, and their capacity to change. And while there's no blueprint for marriage, the seismic shifts that happen when you share a life with someone are an essential part of the human experience. Like many of the friends and acquaintances in our lives who give into the ground opening up beneath their feet, I begin to see these are all ways we surrender in order to survive, and I get it. There's no blueprint for survival. There's no one way to love, or to live.

A queer spirituality gives us a way to live out these relationships more courageously, more openly, more meaningfully, with a different kind of joy and hope. We can live with the realization that there is no guarantee and not everything lasts forever, but what we make of our time, and with whom, matters. Queering intimacies means I can make that choice, and I do every day—to love and be loved.

***

It's a Tuesday morning. Andy heads into work early. After I drop the kids off at school, Andy leaves his office and meets me in the lobby of a building downtown. We have another appointment with our therapist. Andy greets me with a quick peck on the cheek, and we step into the elevator together, catching up—figuring out who will go to the store later to get food for dinner or who will make the phone call to the utilities company. Maybe we hold hands. When we get to the therapist's office, she opens the door with a smile. I sit down on the couch next to a large green houseplant in a vase. I mindlessly finger its leaves while sinking into the cushions, and Andy settles into the armchair adjacent to me. While the therapist pulls out a notebook, she sits in her chair across from us and starts out with the same question she uses each time: "How are you?"

We look at each other and take a deep breath, letting the threads of what we held onto unravel in our hands as we make something new between us.

Notes

1. Elisabeth Elliot, "Marriage: A Revolution and a Revelation," 2010, PDF, https://tinyurl.com/ycnw3ecn.

2. Act of Feb. 10, 1855, 10 Stat. 604, as reenacted in Revised Statutes of the U.S. (1878), sect. 1994.

3. John Bonazzo, "A Biology Teacher Just Destroyed Every Excuse for Transphobia with Cold, Hard Facts," *Observer*, March 3, 2017, https://tinyurl.com/y9vh5y7h.

6

Keeping It in the Family

Your children are not your children.
They are sons and daughters of Life's longing for itself.
They come through you but not from you.
And though they are with you yet they belong not to you.

—Khalil Gibran

I was a tomboy. Until I reached my midtwenties, my typical outfit was knee-length (usually cargo) shorts and graphic T-shirts, sometimes punctuated with a baseball cap and flip-flops. I never wore makeup and hardly did my hair except to wear it long and stick-straight. As a child, I was always covered head to toe in grime, scrapes and bruises, and more often than not, dried blood.

My parents bemoaned my lack of girlish sensibilities. On the day of my seventh birthday, as I waited for my friends' arrival to celebrate the occasion, I tried to do handstands on the driveway. My elbow buckled on one attempt, and I scraped my cheek on the concrete. When I ran into the house, crying, my mother shook her head at me as she dabbed the wound clean. Clicking her tongue, annoyed, she said, "You're wearing a dress; why are you playing like a boy?"

"You're too wild," my parents said. They urged me, "Be normal, be like a girl," because I wasn't quiet and delicate like other girls.

Even at church, in a dress or skirt, I would play and get in trouble. Though I was mostly dutiful, I couldn't sit still for very long. As a way to channel that energy, adults would call on me to help in the kitchen or to set out the plasticware for lunch after the worship service. But as soon as I was allowed, I joined the other kids to start a game of hide-and-seek—of course, always after pausing to *in-sa*, or bow in greeting, to the church elders or deacons, calling them by their proper titles in Korean before I scampered past them in the church stairways.

When I entered middle school, my father sought to tame my wild ways by making me work at the church even more. I obediently played the piano during the hymn sing—an hour set aside before worship, when church members would arrive early and pick songs to sing. My father directed that time, and I tried to keep my eyes zeroed in on him, even as my fingers meticulously pounded on the keys. But inevitably, my eyes would wander to the door leading outside. In response, he would emphatically tap out the tempo with a pencil on a music stand, so I wouldn't play too slow or too fast. Afterward, I would run downstairs for the youth-group service held during morning worship, and like a good daughter of the church, I helped babysit the younger children and taught

Sunday school to the elementary-school kids. I was always the big sister. But when we were done, we would play basketball or look for insects to spring on our moms in the kitchen, who would squeal at us to go back outside, where we would fall over laughing.

Be normal. This was normal to me. Day in and day out, Monday through Friday, I would live a certain way, trying to navigate so many cultural clashes and collisions of worlds. It felt like I was holding my breath. But then on Sundays, I would exhale, with my parents, my family all around me, and I would sing and breathe and laugh a little more easily.

We reify and conserve the "normal" in all sorts of ways. Family is one of the cultural sites in which our deeply held values are most powerfully lived out by words, gestures, and even the place where we sit at the dining table. In these spaces, our values are enforced, reproduced, and normalized. For much of Western civilization, the idea of "normal" is rooted in a narrow understanding of gender and sexuality that presumes the preferred norm is to be cisgender—having a gender identity that matches the gender assigned at birth—and heterosexual. For example, children are viewed not only as offspring but also as legacies, inheritors of these standards and priorities, and are treated not only as the future laborers of our institutions but as the actual building blocks. Children are a means in which we establish cisgendered and heterosexual norms. Numerous markets—economic and religious—center the existence of children and the proliferation of civilization through education, entertainment, and a host of tangible products. Look at the clothing options, toys, and party supplies for boys and girls in any Target. Whether it's the content of t-shirts like NASA for boys but only pretty, flowery ones for girls or building and construction toys for boys and dolls for girls, children are compelled to see and desire a particular identity as it fits the gendered norms within a family. Like most people on the margins in a capitalist society, children are stripped of agency and often treated like commodities. Not only are they acted upon but they are used to buttress notions of the "perfect" family.

But, there is no such thing as the perfect family—perfect marriages, perfect parents, perfect sons and daughters. Still, we often conflate perfect and normal.

What's "normal" is in the air we breathe. My family and my church (which was my people, my tribe, an extension of my family when I was growing up) constantly sought to perpetuate a certain identity for me, expressed through language, clothing, and certain jobs, even as I tried to resist it all in conscious and unconscious ways. Recognizing this as a parent today, I try to pay attention to the ways I fall into certain practices with my own children and with the young people in my church and community. But despite my best intentions, nearly everything in my parenting is connected to normalizing certain acceptable roles for gender, race, sexuality, class, ability, and more.

Sometimes I think the traditional family unit is just another way to normalize certain values through assimilation. Yet everywhere I look within my own family, I see queerness constantly hovering on the edges of my vision—in parenting, working, and maintaining and sustaining a home life. Expanding notions of "family" can contribute to the wider good and contribute to a different notion of normal.

The Value of Family Values

Much of my extended family lives in South Korea. When we immigrated to the United States, we moved to Colorado Springs, Colorado, where my mother's sister lived with her family. We spent nearly every weekend with my cousins, and between them and our local Korean Presbyterian church, it felt like we had a large family. Though I had met my grandparents only a handful of times (we went to Korea twice as a family, my father's parents visited us once, and my mother's mother came a few times), I didn't pay too much attention to this lack, even when my friends in high school would tell me about their annual visits to their grandparents in the summers. Instead, every Sunday felt like a family reunion, replete with food, stories, and raucous laughter. All generations were present, from gurgling babies to grandmothers who would dote on you and the solemn grandfathers who, like my grandfather, would silently and bemusedly look on all the chaos in the fellowship hall.

We lived on the north side of the city, near James Dobson's organization, Focus on the Family, founded by Dobson in 1976. Its sprawling campus seemed to grow by leaps and bounds every year. By the time I earned my bachelor's degree and went back home for a year, I even had a few college friends who participated in a popular semester-long program on apologetics there. Focus on the Family's curriculum, seminars, radio shows, conferences, and robust website gave—and still gives—the organization an extensive reach.

Although many Christian organizations, from Compassion International to Young Life, made Colorado Springs their central hub, Focus on the Family's presence was the most deeply felt in the city. The organization's message was simple, easily and readily consumed. It was all about the family, and specifically, the traditional nuclear family—one father, one mother, and at least two, if not more, children. This is the shiny center of the image of the American dream. Who wouldn't sign on to this? When we immigrated to the United States, my parents signed on to it without realizing, and they consumed it whole, bones and blood. The family—patriarchal, traditional, and Christian—was the center of everything.

Currently, across the top of its home page, Focus on the Family's website declares this slogan: "Helping Families Thrive." The organization's mission statement articulates six values: evangelism, marriage, children, sanctity of life, social responsibility, and "The Value of Male and Female." The brilliance of their marketing lies in how they name the reality that sustaining marriage and family is hard, even as they promise that they have the answer. And their answer is that as long as everyone lives, breathes, and acts within their set, *designed* role, everyone will be happy, and our society will thrive, and all will be and feel fulfilled. All of these perspectives were interwoven into my family life, church life, and community life. They were felt everywhere from the hall-ways of my school to the streets of my suburban neighbor-hood.

Many modern-day civilizations emphasize marriage between a man and a woman as foundational to an indus-trialized society in which labor and capital depend on the production of offspring. Marriage as an institution—whether secular or religious—lifts up heterosexuality and heterosexual relationships as the norm. *Christian* marriage takes it a step further, solidifying heteronormativity by promoting the idea that marriage between a man and woman is actually blessed by God—sacred and holy. It's the vehicle that propagates civ-ilization, and even more so, *Christian* civilization.

We could put this bluntly: the evangelical Christian perspective is that more Christian marriages equal more Christian babies and families, and that equals more Christian communities ushering in the kingdom of God. Focus on the Family says it this way:

> We believe that the institution of marriage is a sacred covenant designed by God to model the love of Christ for His people and to serve both the public and private good as the basic building block of human civilization. Marriage is intended by God to be a thriving, lifelong relationship between a man and a woman enduring through trials, sickness, financial crises and emotional stresses. Therefore, Christians are called to defend and protect God's marriage design and to minister in Christ's name to those who suffer the consequences of its brokenness.[1]

Religious dogma and matters of eternity were a part of the special evangelical formula for opposing anything that would threaten the idea of heterosexual and monogamous marriage.

Any glimmering expression of a relationship outside the proper bounds of marriage was the ultimate threat not just to Christianity, but to the very existence of humanity. This principle actually squared quite well with my parents' Korean, Confucian values. We can't raise good, God-fearing children unless the family was fixed and rooted in the Christian foundation of marriage. Ultimately, it's the offspring that gives family, and especially heteronormative marriage, its purpose.

Sexuality and procreativity are inseparable.

Yet, not all cultures uphold the familiar ideals of heterosexual monogamy as the center of their identity. The Naxi People of Lugu Lake are a fascinating community who practice a type of matrilineal family called *yidu* (meaning house). The community relies on the concept of *azhu* (which means friend or partner). Within pairings of *azhus*, each partner continues to live at home, and they do not establish a new family together. Each works for and supports their respective mother's family; the offspring belong to the mother and are her responsibility. The ties between partners can last for several years or for one or two nights, because each partner is free to sever the relationship or continue it and to have any number of other relations. The more attractive and intelligent members of the society have several partners, and it is a source of pride and respect, while those who are less appealing usually have one *azhu*. This is an early form of group marriage and one of the last vestiges of it in the world.[2] The Naxi show us that the value of family is not limited to the nuclear family or to the Christian family. Communities thrive and perpetuate through other configurations, and when we allow for these possibilities—for diversity, as in any ecosystem—we encourage life.

The conservative discourse around "biblical marriage" naturally extends to the family, creating a narrow and limited understanding. It prevents us from seeing all the iterations of family around us, whether it's single parent or multiple parents, whether it's single children or multiple children. We see that hardly anything in the Bible actually matches the contemporary notion of the nuclear family. In the Bible, we find Jacob with his many wives, concubines, twelve sons, and one daughter; Solomon with his hundreds of wives and children; Hannah abandoning her son Samuel to the temple and forgoing any further influence on his life; the Gospels' portrayal of the disciples, apostles, and Jesus with no mention of their family lives; and the New Testament letters' emphasis on celibacy. The concept of a two-spouse nuclear family is not cut-and-dried. Rather, so-called "biblical" principles are actually piecemeal Scripture passages craftily strung together. Using these as the basis for a single legitimate version of family not only devalues the witness of the Scriptures but also dilutes the daily, gracious possibility of family truly being a space that teaches the full value of humanity.

The value of family, whether each one is birthed, fostered, adopted, or appointed, is not in its capacity to mindlessly further the human species through rote duplication or reiteration. We're not trying for perfect automatons, and the goal shouldn't be cookie-cutter, like the suburban development we are currently making our home, where trees occupy the sidewalks in precise lines and the same flower pots hang on every porch. The value is in admitting the struggle without shame and in not squeezing every member of the family into an abstract ideal or "biblical principle." It's in the beautifully chaotic space of creating. It's messily becoming through a love that multiplies itself by leaps and bounds with grace always present at the door.

Let the Children Lead

From the moment my children entered my life, they broke open a part of me that feels for other human beings in a way I'd never experienced before. I don't think it's necessary to have children in order to be empathetic, but that is exactly what needed to happen to me. Every person is someone's child, and what is happening to those who are marginalized, those of another religious background, black and brown babies, children raised in economically disadvantaged areas, and LGBTQIA youth, hits me hard.

I'm daily haunted by the statistics on LGBTQIA youth. According to the Centers for Disease Control and Prevention (CDC), anywhere from a quarter to a third of LGBT students experience bullying on school property or electronically, and a little less have experienced physical or sexual violence. And this is just what is disclosed by the survey respondents. Up to 1.6 million youth experience homelessness each year. The statistics for LGBT homeless youth are even more shocking, as this group represents up to 40 percent of all young people experiencing homelessness. Considering that LGBT youth represent an estimated 7 percent of the total youth population, these numbers are disproportionately high. While even a single young person without a home is one too many, the disparity of LGBT youth experiencing homelessness is unfathomable.[3]

Suicide is the third leading cause of death among youth ages fifteen to twenty-four, and LGBT youth are more likely to attempt suicide than their straight peers. Recent population-based studies suggest that the reported rates of suicide attempts for high-school students who identify as LGBT are two to seven times higher than rates among high-school students who describe themselves as heterosexual. LGBT youth are also twice as likely to have thoughts about suicide.[4]

Like most parents, I think often about how to protect my children from anything that would destroy their sense of worth, dignity, and value; how to teach them to trust the ones that love them; and how to lead them to see that they have agency and that their voices, perspectives, words, and stories are important. To try to understand my children as individuals, I observe them, regularly, and the collection of stories about my children is endless.

One morning, they came downstairs growling and hissing, gliding on all fours. Desmond's arm bent out a little, and he stumbled down the rest of the stairs on his face. "Wahhhhh, Mommmmmmy, I fell down and hit my face!" he cried.

I ran over and paused as he stretched out his hands toward me. They were red. The children had decided they would be jaguars, since "jaguars have spots" (do they have spots???), and *no wonder* it had been so quiet for fifteen minutes. They had been coloring their faces and appendages with, thankfully, washable markers—red for Desmond, and blue, green, and purple for Anna. Both looked more like alien creatures than anything we would see on the Planet Earth series.

Ozzie got in on it, and the three of them passed the rest of the morning playing jaguars—lunging at each other and running away, rolling and wrestling, swiping and clawing like blind kittens just born into this world. Walking on hands and feet proved to be much more difficult than they had anticipated, I think, as they lumbered around with measured steps. "Mommy, do jaguars have stripes? Do leopards have stripes?" Desmond asked, as he parsed out the differences in cats.

"No, tigers have stripes, dear," I said to him.

"Oh." He thought this over, clearly debating with himself whether he should get markers and make some revisions on his body. But when he saw my disapproving look, it preempted those thoughts: "Uh, yeah, okay, I want to be a tiger. Later."

Later that day, a sweet boy named Sebastian came to summer camp wearing a Queen Elsa (from the movie *Frozen*) dress. On his feet were Crocs featuring Queen Elsa and Princess Anna. My Anna asked why he was wearing a dress. "Boys don't wear dresses," she said, more as a question. "Boys and girls can wear whatever makes them feel happy," I responded, a little too loudly, so all could hear. And for emphasis, I added, "Plus, doesn't he look so pretty? I think the blue looks nice on him." She didn't notice my awkwardness, but just nodded and smiled.

When I picked up the kids at the end of the day, Anna told me every detail of the day. They painted and made doughnut holes, and she pulled someone in a wagon, and they pulled her, too, and she, Sebastian, Ozzie, and Desmond pretended they were lions, but then Ivan kicked Desmond in the face and kicked her in the face, and Sebastian told Ivan that he shouldn't do that, because it's not nice. "He's a good boy," she concluded.

In the evening, we went to the preschool for one of their many annual plays. The twins hated plays. While the rest of the kids crooned at the top of their lungs, yelled, and stomped around onstage, gesticulating wildly, Anna stood in a corner and pensively stared out into the audience. Desmond stretched his body out on the stage behind all the kids and looked as though he was preparing to nap. We stood near the stage with them to reassure them, and their teachers held their hands to try to get them to participate with the others. They refused.

Later we asked the twins, "Why didn't you sing the songs or say your lines?" They only shrugged as if to say, "What songs? What play?" And I felt this weird pressure inside, wondering, *Why do the other kids sing and play and act like kids, and not ours? What am I doing wrong? Am I a bad parent?*

That question haunts me all day long: *Am I a bad parent?* I worry sometimes that people look at me and wonder the same thing. I worry I will be caught and people will know that I am a terrible parent, or that I'm not doing enough, or that I'm doing it wrong. How am I passing for a parent? Because let's get it straight, I have no idea what the hell I'm doing most of the time.

As humans, we are constantly passing, that is, working to make our identities palatable and intelligible to the wider world. Historically, the term was used in the United States to describe a person of multiracial ancestry assimilating into the white majority, especially when being classified as a minority made a person subject to racial segregation and discrimination. Today, this is a way to talk about how people with any marginalized identities move through spaces, namely through white, heteronormative ones.

The concept of passing goes hand-in-hand with new and improved notions about identity. Passing upends all our tidy little methods of categorizing human beings and makes us wonder what exactly makes an identity authentic, or whether and how authenticity matters.

These days, the ideals of "authenticity" and "identity" have begun to unravel for me. They are not tied up together in the same way. And I wrestle with what we mean by it, why exactly it matters, and how we are to judge it in another person. What does it mean to take on an identity and to find meaning in and through it? I look at my kids in their rainbow-colored stripes and spots, and boys in their princess dresses. What I see is that they are playing, and they are happy. Even if they are on stage and not performing in the same way as all the other kids, they are occupying that space in their own peculiar and lovely way.

Queering Family Values

In many Korean immigrant communities, children and youth have a community virtually separate from the adults, particularly when it comes to Sunday worship. This meant we never saw any baptisms, and we barely participated in the Lord's Supper. When I took Communion for the second time in college at the local Presbyterian church, I felt an acute sadness that I hadn't been able to experience it more with my family when I was a child. The impact of these exclusionary practices never struck me until I realized how much I'd missed out.

One of the few times for the inclusion of children in my home church came during the Christmas Eve service, because it included a children's Christmas play. And while it is easy to critique Christian institutions for the siloing of children, especially in the ways we unintentionally prop them up for our own entertainment, there was something subversive happening onstage. Children were allowed to shape and occupy the worship space in whatever way inspired their fancy. We were given relatively free rein. In this way, through story and song, we challenged the regular perceptions of identity.

We did a play every year around the Christmas themes. I loved the exhilaration of performing for our parents, even though obnoxious Elder Lee would always shout at us from the pews in Korean, "Didn't you eat breakfast?" It was a cultural way to say, "Speak up! We can't hear you." We'd laugh, always embarrassed by the interruption, but it never totally took away from the strange, lovely feeling of enacting the nativity story.

Sometimes we would perform in Korean, and you could see the parents' faces light up as they heard the words. Sometimes we used English, with someone translating in Korean, summarizing what happened in each scene, and I could see all our parents strain a little more to pay attention. Sometimes we would interchange Korean and English, and it was an odd mix of the silly and nonsensical, with puns that played off both languages. Usually, girls would play the shepherds or even the three wise men, because there were always more girls than boys.

Joseph was always a boy, and Mary was always a girl. One of the girls in our church who was multiracial—Korean and white—would often play Mary. It was as if she was the only one who could pass for her, like she was the one who looked most like the Mary in our children's Bibles, with her dewy brown eyes and long eyelashes. Or it would be the older, good Korean girl who spoke perfect Korean, was pretty, was the cheerleader, was the girly girl, and sang beautifully.

One year, I played the angel Gabriel, and the thought crossed my mind that angels are neither boys nor girls. It was this ambiguity that oddly assuaged any stage fright as I sang my first solo. There was no expectation of whether I was a girl or boy or Korean or white. I focused on playing a messenger of God, which was what mattered the most. These performances of the nativity story ever so slightly shifted the way we all experienced the world—all of us, young and old, first and second generation, black and Korean and white. We were able to act out in bodies and voices those things that on a regular day would invite a heavy chastening. Children in drag. Boys draped in wings and long shimmery dresses sang in choirs of angels. Girls donned beards and crowns and played the shepherds or wise men. Their voices rang out, proclaiming the good news of Jesus's birth, from a space that normally allowed only males to preach and teach. As a result, there was a flattening effect: the normal hierarchies that structured the community disintegrated as our bodies presented new identities.

It is an incarnational work to enter into or create ritualistic spaces mediated by our physical bodies, our faces, our hair, our skin and clothes, and all our bodily expressions. This is how we engage in identity making.

Performing, passing, playing—none of this negates the authenticity of our words, actions, and relationships. Yet, recognizing that we are all "playing"—acting and passing—helps us see the insidious scripts that penetrate all of our lives, whether we are aware of them or consent to them. The various places and groups we occupy often burst at the seams with expectations for how we are to act in relation to each other. But sometimes those lines get unexpectedly blurred by the subversive lights of Christmas trees and sanctuaries, where girls are wise men and humans are angels. Ultimately, these spaces are still burdened by our systems of definitions and identifying, and by our need to draw lines in the sandbox. But a playful and holy disruption can cause a breach in what's normal, opening a window into other possibilities.

The sanctuary of Andy's church has two huge stained-glass windows that seem to bookend the chancel. On one side is an image of the post-resurrection Jesus appearing to Mary in the garden. On the other side, we see Jesus surrounded by children, one in his lap, and all their mothers hovering nearby.

Much of what Jesus did was shocking, and the story of Jesus welcoming the children was no less. Perhaps the disciples were tired and ready to be done attending to the crowds' many, many needs. And these were children, after all—dirty, sticky with juice and urine, faces smeared with snot and left-over breakfast. Jesus had no obligation to look at them, much less talk to them or touch them. It was getting late, and everyone was hungry and ready for a bath. So the disciples tried to move them along, these parents who came for Jesus's blessing on their children. But Jesus reprimanded the disciples and reminded them that the keys to the kingdom are found in these children.

Queerness is the recognition that we are all passing for something as we work out our identities and relationships. By virtue of being human, we are constantly learning about ourselves and therefore pressing up against the boundaries of gender, race, and ultimately the definition of *human*. Sometimes we perform our identities—who we think we are, what we feel on the inside—and sometimes not. Sometimes we see identity and can read it, and sometimes not, but that doesn't make it any less real or authentic. A queer spirituality upends what we think is normal and leads us to find the beauty in what might seem weird and strange. I have found freedom in playing—freedom from the way I understand myself, my relationships, and even my parenting—because if there is one thing I love about parenting, it is that 90 percent of it is playing. Through playing, we explore, we challenge, we love, and we bless.

Notes

1. Focus on the Family, "Foundational Values," https://tinyurl.com/y9kdjkt9.
2. "The Naxi People of Lugu Lake," *China Pictorial* 2 (1980): 8–15.
3. True Colors Fund, "Our Issue," https://tinyurl.com/yczd4an7.
4. "Behavioral Health," youth.gov, https://tinyurl.com/y8ezojy3.

7

The Friend Zone

See, when a girl decides you're her friend, you're no longer a
dating option—you become a complete nonsexual entity in her
eyes. Like a brother. Or a lamp.

—Chris Bander, *Just Friends*

I wouldn't call myself movie connoisseur, but I can't resist the
chance to talk about the film *Just Friends*. And I'll take any
chance I have to talk about Ryan Reynolds and Amy Smart
and to rewatch clips of Ryan Reynolds. Because he's incredibly funny, and they're both super hot.

Now, *Just Friends* is exactly what you'd imagine a movie
like this is about—the friend zone, that strange, liminal, often-
confusing space that is the center of angsty observations by
everyone from Seinfeld to long-ago famous Christian writers
like Joshua Harris of *I Kissed Dating Goodbye* (Harris references the friend zone in only an oblique way). Ryan Reynolds
and Amy Smart play Chris and Jamie, best friends from high
school, and of course, Chris is in love with Jamie. At
the end of their senior year, he is humiliated after his romantic

declaration is discovered in her yearbook and then read aloud by her current boyfriend to everyone at a party. She doesn't reciprocate, so Chris leaves, dejected. After some years pass, he moves on to become successful, cool, incredibly attractive, and a womanizer. Through the magic of movie storytelling, he somehow ends up back in his hometown, where he reunites with Jamie, only to find those old feelings surface again. The story is a back-and-forth, he-said/she-said whirlwind with side characters who complicate the narrative, but predictably, in the end, the guy gets the girl. Chris escapes the friend zone, and that is, apparently, the ultimate goal.

I can't think of a single movie where the guy *doesn't* get the girl but they remain friends. If such movies exist, they are few and far between. We live in a culture that idolizes stories about the prince getting the princess or sometimes a pseudo-feminist vice versa. Either way, it's the myth that one's destiny is somehow fulfilled totally and completely in another person.

The friend zone is rarely a desired position, and not just for those sex-crazed or even mildly sex-interested individuals who are trying to get past the platonic into someone's pants, as it is often portrayed in the typical rom-com. Moreover, it is a position that is looked at negatively by those who believe they need to follow the script and move toward that ultimate relationship: one that is monogamous and procreative. According to this script, friendship only gets you so far, though it is a good place to start. I've certainly discovered in my own marriage, and observed in other couples, that friendship is a good foundation for one's forever relationship. But, it's hardly ever considered as an end in itself. Friendships are usually seen as peripheral, superficial, and utilitarian—necessary only to a certain level and only within a certain framework. They're just not as important as the spousal relationship.

These days, I have found a deep sense of identity and wholeness in queer friendships, that is, friendships that blur the typical boundaries. My hope is that we will embrace "friendship, not coupled love," as the *normative* adult human relationship, where "friendship undergirds [all] our commitments."[1]

I'm reminded that most historical treatments of friendship aren't terribly robust. They likely find their roots in Greek thinkers like Aristotle, and in fact, many of the early Greek writings were unsurprisingly focused on the male–male friendship. The thinking at the time was that females weren't mentally, emotionally, and intellectually evolved enough to have friendships in the same way. But in general, the beginning glimmerings of life for the early Christians in the Greco-Roman world was markedly different when it came to friendships, relationships, and marriages, and certainly when it came to men and women.

I digress, slightly. What's useful for us is the reminder that these shifts around relationships constantly happen throughout history—sometimes implicitly, in corners and hidden rooms, and sometimes, explicitly, through stories and policies. These queer shifts in understanding the vital role of friendship invite me to organize my daily life intentionally around my connections with others. Friendship is not a second-tier, perfunctory kind of interaction. Imagine how our lives would be transformed if we took seriously that friendship is the necessary base for every possible relationship.

In other words, to queerly pursue the friend zone is good and right, because that is an experience that rounds out who I am as a person. A queer spirituality fills in the gaps; it shapes me in ways that one single relationship cannot, even if that one relationship is marriage.

Friends Are Friends Forever

My senior year in high school, our class voted for *Friends* as our class TV show. I'm having trouble remembering whether the class song was the theme song from *Friends* or Michael W. Smith's "Friends Are Friends Forever." Either one is equally painful for their levels upon levels of cliched sentimentality.

It has taken me a long time to understand friendship—what it means to have friends, to be a friend, and to have a friend. At the very least, when I was young, I knew that I was only supposed to be friends with girls. Somehow, I knew early on what was *appropriate*, whether it was taught by parents or simply present in the air all around us. There were appropriate things to do or say, appropriate people to play with, and appropriate clothes and colors to wear.

Now, with our children, I try to define and model all kinds of friendship. We might talk about best friends, friends who are boys or girls, and more terrifyingly, girlfriends and boyfriends. Even at this young age, our children are aware of the various levels of connection, and their friendships are truly fluid and almost seasonal. Some weeks, Desmond will talk about one or two boys he plays with every single day, and then we don't hear about them for a while. Anna has her best friend, but she is also able to connect with a wide range of kids. Sometimes they tell me stories about little squabbles or hurt feelings. One day, Anna told me how she got her best friend to do everything for her that day. "Friendship is give-and-take, Anna," I said. "You have to take turns doing things for each other," trying to help her not only have a friend but *be* a friend.

That's what it seems like it's mostly about in the beginning: not learning how to get or collect friendships, but just figuring out how to *be* a friend. The lessons are simple things like asking a person's name (the kids often would come home excited about making a friend but unable to remember the other child's name) and then memorizing it. Or they had to learn to ask questions like *What's your favorite color?* and *What's your favorite animal?* as a way to show interest and offer a welcome.

But for all the talk of friendship with my kids, making friends was never really natural or easy for me. That is why, when I was Anna's age, I found myself befriending more boys than girls. Every year, my best friend was a boy, up until we moved to Denver when I was in fourth grade. Joe, Tim, Jason, Shelby—I just never found myself in a circle of girl friends. I had a BFF here and there, and I connected with people who were often from different groups—jocks, nerds, musicians. I engaged each of these interesting individuals in particular ways. I felt like groups of girlfriends seemed cliché, like something out of a TV show or, later, undesirable and terrifying à la *Mean Girls*. Yet I secretly longed for that circle, desiring it for a long time, even as I got older—to be surrounded by laughter at inside jokes and stories told around a table full of food and wine, like a scene from *Sex and the City*. It seemed glamorous and rich.

Even in college, when I lived with groups of girls, though we became close and I felt known and loved by them (some of them were even my bridesmaids), I never quite felt that gelling, that ride-or-die feeling, that feeling of totally belonging. I always felt a little off, a little queer. In seminary, I had a few close friends and many acquaintances, and I was generally social. Still, there was no group or community setting where I felt totally at ease, as if I totally fit.

And then I became a mother. I joined mom groups, because motherhood was so lonely and isolating that first year. It was confusing, disorienting, and it goes without saying, exhausting. To be together with other mothers and children on a regular basis for playdates sustained my emotional and spiritual sanity. Even if it was just two moms with our gaggle of babies, at the very least another being with an adult body and mind was nearby, and I could actually have a conversation with someone over two feet tall. There were other children to play with (read: entertain and distract) my children, and this was lifesaving. And the playdates brought the continuous profound reminder that I wasn't alone. When I let myself be taken care of and loved, something new opened up within me. I discovered that when my children were cared for, I felt that care, too. I was bewildered by this new sensation—to be seen, heard, cared for, and loved so deeply by friends.

Perhaps something about having children softened me and made me live in community a little differently. Strangely, paying attention to my child's incessant needs also let me recognize my own neediness and then be okay with feeling needy. That's something I never grew up seeing as okay. Being needy was for babies, for children, and maybe for our parents toward the end of their lives. Trying to demonstrate some semblance of unwavering strength closed me off to the world, but motherhood opened me up again.

Molly Wizenberg, author and blogger at *Orangette* resonates:

> I think the shift started, millimeter by millimeter, when June was born. Having a baby, having her, softened me. It broke me a little. It gave me first-hand knowledge of the fullness of joy and the emptiness of clinical depression. It made me appreciate my body, and femaleness, in a new way. It committed me to becoming the kind of person I want June to know and remember and be proud of. It committed me to being a person I want to parent her. It made me brave.[2]

When the twins were just born, I would be measuring out formula to supplement the breastfeeding, and it felt as if I were living out the days in millimeters and minutes. But these tiny moments were creating small cracks in my hard exterior. I didn't realize the small chunks that felt like they were being chiseled out of my soul were carving out a different way for me to be in the world. For Molly, this led to some revelations about marriage and about herself (she discovered a change in her sexual orientation, came out, and is now newly partnered). For me, I finally embraced that it is more than okay to need others—especially my friendships, my sisters, my tribes. The mom group here in town was a lifeline, and there are women both near and far who have known and loved me through some of the darkest seasons of my life as I lived into motherhood. Something about parenthood makes finding connection effortless. A group of Asian American clergywomen have sustained me as I navigated another kind of loneliness and isolation in the intersecting questions of parenthood, vocation, and specifically, racial identity. Being a woman-of-color professional in any field simply can't be done without a network of similarly situated companions, even if they're hundreds of miles away.

Lately, one important community to me is a group of women who were convened by two powerhouse women speakers, who have now become dear friends to me. They enabled our voices, as individuals and as a collective, and encouraged a space where women fiercely love and advocate for one another. We shine together. There are so many ways to be open to their love and care for me, and to the methods they use to express their loyalty and faithfulness: phone calls, texts, letters, and gifts. But when we're together, face to face and in each others' presence, it's a veritable love feast: we play hard, we love hard, we cuddle, we pray for each other, we sing to each other, we cook for each other, and we make a hedge of protection around each other. We make space for each to be seen, received, affirmed, and held together. And it doesn't stop there as we continue to hold space for each other through phone calls, texts, emails, and other messages, so much so that I don't feel the effects of the physical distance. And thank God, because I can't imagine my life without these women. I can't imagine surviving this world without them. I have no doubt I could call up any one of them at any moment of need, and they would show up at my door.

All friendships, both near and far, feed and boost me in ways that one person can't do, and shouldn't be expected to do, even if that person is your spouse or primary partner. But they all make up a constellation of voices and loving support that sustain the universe within each person. All this might sound like the stuff of romance, but what I've learned is that it is friendship—real, lasting friendship.

Friendship Is the New Romance

Friendship has now become the primary form of relationship for many people, especially women. In *All the Single Ladies: Unmarried Women and the Rise of an Independent Nation*, writer Rebecca Traister talks about friendships between unmarried women becoming the living, supportive structure for their regular lives. She recounts the story of a friend named Sara who had fallen love with a man and moved away to Boston, only to return again after six months. Says Traister, "She came back because the relationship she'd traveled to Boston for wasn't fulfilling. More important, she came back because the life she'd left in New York—her work, her city, her friends—was fulfilling. She came back for herself. She says now that it was a New York job listing that was the beacon: 'It was telling me to return to the life that fed me, my circle of friends, to return to myself.'"[3]

As more women realize there isn't a singular way to create a community of support and stability, and that marriage is simply one option, it appears women are either waiting until much later to marry or else opting out completely. Today 20 percent of Americans ages eighteen to twenty-nine are married, compared with nearly 60 percent in 1960; the median age of first marriage for women has risen to twenty-seven. The marriage rate hit a record low in 2015, and a 2014 Pew Research Center study showed a significant number of adults had never been married and predicted that a quarter of millennials might never marry.

These shifts make sense. No longer is marriage the be-all, end-all to establish one's position in society, especially for women who are gainfully employed with careers and income, and who are secure in their own identities. Marriage isn't the marker or source of fulfillment it once was. This is certainly distinct from the experience of earlier generations, who lived and died by notions that one had to get married and rely on a husband for stability, agency, and really, survival.

Growing up in a traditional Korean Christian home, I

learned early that marriage is the pinnacle relationship. It was hammered home for me everywhere: home, church, the YMCA, and even school and other settings. In many ways, it seemed like any other kind of relationship was subordinate to marriage. It was more than the goal relationship, it was also a marker of adulthood, of maturity, of legitimacy and being taken seriously. But I see now that it was also about putting people in their right roles—putting me in my place. It's not about marriage, really; it was specifically about my becoming a wife someday and fulfilling my duties as a wife. So my parents didn't really encourage friendships outside of the normal interactions at school. We hardly did any playdates and definitely no sleepovers, because cultivating these relationships were ultimately distractions that would prevent me from fulfilling my main role as a wife.

I initially thought friendship was as a natural by-product of marriage, but I have seen that marriage does not make people friends. It creates legal ties that govern shared property, inheritance, and the like. But, a new-to-me idea emerged in conversations when Andy and I began premarital counseling: friendship is a part of healthy marriages. Yet even if we prioritize the idea of becoming friends with a person before becoming their spouse, doing so doesn't erase the same problematic thinking, that is, the idea that everything is about marriage.

However, if we think of friendship as a necessity for marriage, not as secondary or supplemental, but as something embedded in marriage, as equally important to maintain and uphold as the marriage, we frame marriage as a partnership, a relationship of equals. This was revolutionary for me at the time. Soon I heard it everywhere: stories about "marrying your best friend," and this much more than marrying your soul mate. It ended up resonating with what I desired for my own marriage, perhaps because I had felt that something was missing for so long. When Andy and I married, I felt I was marrying someone I knew deeply and who knew me in the same way. Even though we had only known each other for a couple of years, we were best friends. And according to all the literature, this meant that our marriage would be rock solid.

Yet it wasn't always that simple. Marriage didn't solve all the problems. Friendship did help us understand that there are two, self-differentiated individuals in this relationship. We felt confident we could work through anything and everything with mutual respect, trusting that the commitment of friendship and marriage made our relationship more robust. But even our best intentions sometimes got lost in even the most basic conversations about replacing the toothpaste cap or putting away dirty laundry. Maybe that's just part of what is to be human, though.

Still, friendship is complicated by marriage in some ways, and the interplay of friendship, marriage, relationship, romance, sex, and more is incredibly strange. Sometimes the work to sustain a marriage entails the kind of work that is necessary to sustain a friendship. This means respecting boundaries and borders for individuation—to realize that we aren't the core of each other, we won't always have the answers or solutions, and we can't fix it or fix each other.

I always tell people that marriage taught me more about ministry than any seminary class. Marriage has taught me more about an individual's vulnerability and need, that each person has good and bad, and that each person is complicated. But during this most recent decade, my friendships have taught me that romance is not the be-all and end-all, and that a queer spirituality can change the substance of all our relationships. "Friendship," writes Mary Hunt, "includes love and power, embodiment and spirituality."[4] Friendship recognizes that there are boundaries and borders and walls around people. Connection—whether platonic or romantic or intimate—happens when each person consents to allow the other to permeate those lines, whether in physical or emotional ways. It might be a touch, embrace, caress, or simple recognition. These connections are intertwined, and they manifest in unique combinations within each individual friendship.

Friendship is the necessary building block of any social organization or network, whether it's marriage or romance, church or family, school or agency, city or neighborhood. This doesn't mean that friendship has a blueprint. It doesn't mean that complications or conflicts are absent. Commitment to each other's well-being must always be present. This commitment ought not be transactional or conditional, even though we know that this will always be a part of any kind of relationship, because we are human, and everything we say and do is tinged with agenda or condition. Our motives aren't pure. But once we let go of the pressures of purity—this unrealistic expectation to "love unconditionally"—we might find ourselves more and more empathetic and concerned for the other. We might realize that friendship, relationship, and belonging are about more than the superficial, mutual benefits of this kind of commitment. It's how God created us, formed after God's own triune self, God-in-Community. We live into our createdness more wholly and meaningfully when we live openly, honestly, and genuinely within the complicated, even contradictory ways we love each other in friendship.

Queering Belonging

I remember first encountering the concept of the Trinity in my high-school Sunday-school class. I was captivated and then transformed by it—this thought of God not being singular in the way we demarcate our own individual human selves. Social relationships are the center of God's very nature. Belonging is innate to the essence of God. Belonging is key to our own identity as well—something we all seek. One way I've come to think about belonging is in terms of kinship, a concept I borrow from Elizabeth Freeman.[5]

Kinship is all about social relationships and the ways we form attachments, including mating patterns, parenthood, marriage, and other social connections. Kinship is a social and not a biological fact—a matter of culture rather than nature. This early understanding of kinship as social rather than physiological certainly paved the way for later developments in reproductive technologies to modify kinship terminology. Now, what Freeman does with kinship in relating it to queer theory is remind us that kinship is rooted in the corporeal—specifically, in our bodies. Kinship is about our bodies, for we cannot form attachments and relationships outside of our own bodily experience. So kinship matters in the way our bodies matter. We understand and engage kinship "as a repertoire of understandings about the body, from a set of strategies oriented around the body's limitations and possibilities, and it may be produced or constructed, but it is still urgent and tangible."

Our relationships are grounded in bodies, in terms of regular, physical proximity (yes, after all, we live embodied), and also about our emotional, spiritual, mental, intellectual connections. And these are maintained in many ways. I joke with Andy about his bromances. I've blogged about them before, and he wrote about them in the book we wrote together, *Yoked*. It's always so amazing to me that he maintains friendships with guys with the kind of dedication that is really "normally" reserved for only the most devoted of . . . boyfriends. He should win awards, I think. He has these other people in his life in this uncomplicated, genuine way—men and women he loves so deeply, and they love him. Many of them are in other states, but they work hard to support, create, transform, and sustain their attachments in such a way that their lives seem truly embedded within one another's. It's something he has always lived out and something I'm living into more and more these last few years.

Kinship, then, embodied and lived out in imaginative ways, seems to fill in the gaps in the traditional categories of relationship that are especially associated with the purity culture of Christianity, whether these gaps are in family (rooted in language around blood, genetics, and reproduction) or in friendship (limited by specific gender identities). Purity culture isn't just about sex or sexuality; rather, it permeates how we think and talk about individuals, motives, relationships, and whole systems by restricting the categories. It's dogmatic in expression and always political and hierarchical in the way it privileges and imbues specific bodies with power. Some people are pure, while many are not because of what they look like, what they do, and who they love.

In contrast, queer kinship transgresses those boundaries by entering the in-between spaces outside of definition and category, broadening the way we live in relationship to each other. Queer kinship is mixing and mingling, as when my kids take their paints and, instead of using only one color at a time, swirl all the colors together and create new and different colors, ones that don't have names and that reside on the edges of the color spectrum. Though I shared examples from both Andy's and my life, I can only really speak for myself when I reiterate that these friendships, when framed as queer kinship, provide a different kind of belonging—of consent, of interaction, of being loved.

In her book *Families We Choose*, Kath Weston claims that lesbians and gays have families of choice outside of, alongside, or in addition to their biological family. One family I know is made up of lesbian moms who jokingly call themselves "the Coven." Two of the moms were once married, but now each is newly partnered with other women who have their own children. I am always inspired by the way they take care of each other and support all the iterations of family. Although these broader kinship relationships are today increasingly pursued by non-queer people, queer kinship remains neither imitative of biological family nor completely independent of the concept of biological family. It gives queer people, and all people, the freedom to find family where they find belonging.[6]

This kind of belonging is, for me, about togetherness. It reminds me that I can do and be so much more when friendship is at the root of who I am. It's more than just being a friend, but also includes being loved by friends, sisters, brothers, women, and men. It took me a while to realize the depth of potential in friendship relationships; it's so much more than consuming glamorous, expensive brunches or hanging out on a couch in a coffee shop 24/7. More and more, as I go through this life, togetherness is what means the most to me. Our surprising intertwining with others is both productive and reproductive—reproducing and multiplying light and love in all the relationships we have in our lives.

So it is friendship that opens up a space for queer kinship. In turn, queer kinship can transform how we do friendship—helping us imagine friendships that are profoundly dynamic and fluid, and that encourage a different kind of intimacy, belonging, and even faithfulness. Queer kinship helps me recognize the way heteronormative scripts I've internalized have created walls, not only between myself and others but also within myself. Sometimes, these lines between people are misinterpreted as definitions and exacerbate notions of the Other, the stranger, the foreigner, the outsider. Those lines hardened by notions of purity force us to consider only singular, limiting ways of viewing people and flourishing in relationship with others. Queer kinships are actually necessary both for survival and for thriving in this world, for the thriving of the world. When we live into this kind of queer kinship, our connection to others becomes more robust, more life-giving, more loving, and limitless, generative, and hopeful.

A queer spirituality recognizes that kinship is for everyone who desires connections that are creative and dynamic. The borders and boundaries that surround us are tenuous, but ultimately what ties us together is our shared humanity. Queer kinship is about embodying that humanity, the complexity and subjectivity, the messy, gritty glory of it all, and embracing the humanity in each other. When we do, we transform ourselves, as well as our communities, our cities, and our world.

Notes

1. Mary E. Hunt, *Fierce Tenderness: A Feminist Theology of Friendship* (Minneapolis: Fortress Press, 2009), 44.

2. Molly Wizenberg, untitled blog post, *Orangette*, November 30, 2016, https://tinyurl.com/y7zlcrq8.

3. Rebecca Traister, "What Women Find in Friends that They May Not Get from Love," *New York Times*, February 27, 2016 (excerpt from *All the Single Ladies: Unmarried Women and the Rise of an Independent Nation*), https://tinyurl.com/y7hrsgdb.

4. Mary Hunt, "Love Your Friends," in *Queer Christianities: Lived Religion in Transgressive Forms* (New York: New York University Press, 2015), 140.

5. Elizabeth Freeman, "Queer Belongings: Kinship Theory and Queer Theory," in *A Companion to Lesbian, Gay, Bisexual, Transgender, and Queer Studies*, ed. George E. Haggerty and Molly McGarry (Hoboken, NJ: Blackwell, 2007).

6. Kath Weston, *Families We Choose* (New York: Columbia University Press, 2005), 74.

8

All Work Is Play

You have a right to experiment with your life. You will make mistakes. And they are right, too.

—Anaïs Nin

My childhood church rented out space and time from a dying white Presbyterian congregation. It was on the south side of the city in a low-income area that bordered one of the wealthier neighborhoods in the city. As far as church buildings go, it was nondescript. I hardly recall what the exterior of the building looked like; it was white, maybe, or brick. The fellowship hall in the basement had a kitchen and a few partitioned-off classrooms. I do remember the sanctuary. Its entire floor was covered with plush reddish-purple carpeting. Even now, in my mind, I can still see the matted, dark spots in various places down the center aisle. Dirt and all manner of things trekked in on our shoes were ground into the threads. Coffee and mysterious food stains darkened some areas. Sunlight sustained over time lightened the carpet in other places.

The pews themselves were a dark wood and hard—no cushions, no comfort for the stoic Presbyterians who filled them each week. And for the newcomers and the less faithful who forgot to bring them, there were black Bibles and hymnals in Korean and English, filled with the familiar translucent pages that characterized the most sacred books. The walls on either side had clear windows, with no stained-glass depictions of the disciples or popular stories from the Bible, no sheep looking at us forlornly or angels looking down on us with pity.

The chancel area in front was simple, with the Communion table below a large, wooden cross. I don't recall a baptismal font. A plain lectern stood on one side, and a pulpit across from it, accompanied by two large, ornate chairs behind. The choir sat off to the side near the baby grand piano, alongside a mishmash of music stands and small, low tables.

The few times children were allowed in that space for worship—during Christmas pageants, for confirmation, and on some rare, random Sunday, like my father's ordination as an elder—I remember being utterly fascinated by everything happening in the front. The choir filed in, and the music director led them to take their seats together. The pastor and a liturgist would walk to their respective seats. Always in the same seat close to the front was the *gwan-sa*, or "prayer mother," a special title for a matriarch of the church. She was an elderly woman tasked with modeling the most devoted prayer life. I don't remember if there were candles. On a

Communion Sunday (which happened only a few times a year), the table would be covered in a white sheet with stacks of sterling-silver trays underneath, along with the bread and chalice.

During the singing of the hymn before Communion, church elders walked up in somber unison. Wearing white gloves and moving in a meticulously choreographed way, they lifted the sheet off the table and folded it into a perfect square before sitting back down. The pastor intoned a short prayer—nothing like the liturgy I am accustomed to now in worship—and then lifted up the elements. The elders went back up for the trays and then walked carefully down, looking at each step as they passed the elements up and down the pews. Each person took a square piece of bread and a small plastic cup of juice, and I looked around at eyes closed and lips moving in quiet prayer before each person reverently consumed what they had taken. At my family's church, I received Communion only once, at my confirmation. The next time I would receive it was at the local Presbyterian church when I was a college student.

Today I'm flabbergasted when I attend a worship service where every person leading is a man. But as a young person, I never thought this was peculiar, because this reality was so deeply ingrained in me by the maleness of our church's pastor, liturgists, elders, and music directors. It was clear that only men should have access to the chancel, except for the occasional and exceptional female deacon, usually older, who would offer the lengthy people's prayer. The Communion table, the pulpit, the chairs—that entire space felt distinctly masculine. There, the voices were quiet, stoic, and deep, in contrast to the kitchen, which was loud, unruly, and filled with the voices and laughter of the women unleashed. I never questioned it. In fact, later when it was suggested to me that women could not only preach in church but even be ordained to the ministry, I scoffed. The person who suggested that to me was my father, who was a seminary student at the time, having left his career as a financial analyst at a computer company.

My traditional, patriarchal father was radicalized as a feminist before my eyes, and I credit him as the main reason I went to seminary. He was the one who started me on this journey where I experienced major shifts in my faith. While in seminary, teachers and students from a wide variety of backgrounds opened up the possibilities of how I encounter God in the church, especially on Sundays—the way God is represented, theologized, worshipped, and liturgized.

As ministers, we live out the vocation as the week-in and week-out experience of leading worship and paying attention to the liturgy, not only for Sunday mornings, but every day—the daily grind, the work of making hospital visits, conducting Bible studies, and leading mission trips and youth group excursions. All of this is liturgy; the Greek word *leitourgia* means "the work of the people," and all of us participate in this collective work and not only our individual vocations.

But before I understood this broader, communal idea of

vocation, the next step in my journey was to think of the ways that we feminize or masculinize, or en-gender, certain work and the spaces in which we do this work. Then I had to recognize how a queer spirituality challenges and welcomes a new way of experimenting, playing, and living out vocation.

Leading in Drag

When I became ordained about a year after my seminary graduation, donning the large, heavy ministerial robe for the first time in worship, I still felt small, like a child trying to fill out her mother's fanciest heels. Every Sunday was an exercise in finding and feeling my voice, my presence, my authority. I did that by trying out different images of preachers and pastors, including preaching professors, Andy, my father, my father-in-law, and even the fleeting memories I had of Robert Schuller, the famous TV preacher of the Crystal Cathedral we grew up watching on Sunday mornings before church. Obviously, none of these quite fit. Eventually, over the passage of time and with practice every week, I found the balance between being my fully unique and in-the-flesh self and being an ordained minister, so that there was hardly a boundary between the two realities. In many ways, they bled into each other, continuously giving new life to myself and ministry.

These days, though I am not serving a church, I will still put on the robe for the periodic Sunday worship. But when I participate in clergy leadership roles, I usually wear the simple clerical collar and shirt, which is a recently adopted practice for me. There is an interesting history behind clergy wear. In the earliest days of Christianity, during the first century, the common dress of the Middle East was robes, though that trend shifted as Christianity spread to Europe, where robes weren't particularly practical in snow and inclement weather. Yet clergy continued to wear the robe as a mark of reverence.

Contrary to what many people might assume, pulpit gowns didn't originate with the Roman Catholic church; rather, they were originally worn by monks, then ministers in the ancient church, and again by Protestant pastors from the time of the Reformation and for hundreds of years thereafter. These robes were different, however, from those of Roman Catholic priests. Instead of a plain gown worn in the pulpit, Roman Catholic priests began wearing very elaborate and ornate robes with complex symbols, known as vestments. This practice came from, as well as promoted, the notion of the priest being above the congregation.

During the sixteenth century, the Reformers sought to correct this view of the priesthood; authority in the church is ministerial authority, not magisterial authority. To that end, the Reformers sought to do away with vestments and simply wore plain black preaching robes, later known as "Genevan gowns," affirmed by the likes of the great Reformer Martin Bucer, who saw the priest and pastor as the servant of the congregation, and determined he should dress as such. Reformed and Presbyterian ministers since the sixteenth century regularly wore the Genevan gown whenever leading worship. The evidence—both written and artistic—reveals that men in the seventeenth and eighteenth centuries all wore pulpit gowns whenever they led worship. Wearing some kind of clergy robe is now the norm, especially in many mainline, Protestant congregations.

The clergy robe I have is usually balled up in the corner of my home office or hanging in the front hall closet with the kids' shoes. Sometimes it's in the trunk of one of the cars, forgotten after I've filled the pulpit for a pastor on vacation. When I stepped down from ministry because of the twins' arrival in 2011, I didn't preach again until Andy's installation service to his current pastoral call. At that point, it had been almost a year since I had stood in the pulpit and ten months since I had stepped onto the chancel. It was strange slipping into the robe, feeling the weight of the cloth resting on my shoulders and hanging down almost to my ankles, getting used to the huge bell sleeves, and fixing the hook at the top of the collar. The stole around my neck shifted often and was in need of constant adjustment. I forgot how wearing the robe was basically like being in a walking sauna, and I was sweating so much by the end of the service. The hook at the collar always has a tendency to come undone, and I forgot to keep checking it. I was delighted to find some cough drops and a tube of cherry ChapStick in the pocket. Wearing the robe was like seeing an old friend. Until it was on, I hadn't realized how much I missed it, and I actually felt a little weepy.

There's something about this marker of the ministerial office—the black robe. The more I think about it, the whole clergy getup strikes me as kind of, well, hilarious. At one ordination service, I watched as numerous ministers went up to lay hands for prayer on the new minister. It appeared to me that these bodies covered in those formidable black robes ultimately looked like disembodied heads floating around the sanctuary, like an alien species. I laughed to myself while I watched their bowed, graying heads with the fascination of a scientist studying its subject from behind a tree.

As I started my own first call as a minister, what tripped me up was the gender identity associated with the robe. What did it look like, sound like, smell like, and taste like to be a minister, beyond putting on the robe? It still felt distinctly male, even though I had seen at least a handful of women clergy leading worship. Whenever I put the robe on, I felt pressure to dilute any feminine presentation. I pulled my hair up and back in a bun, and I wore light makeup, small earrings, and uninteresting black heels. I felt I had to perform in a masculine way for my body, my face and voice, and my actual calling to be acceptable and intelligible to the congregation. I interpreted this to mean stoic, emotionless, serious, cerebral, and with as booming a voice as I could muster on an early Sunday morning. I constantly wrestled with visibly "becoming" masculine and male through clothing and performance, yet whenever I looked down at the robe, I saw that what I wore was more like a dress than anything else.

We talk, we sing, we preach, and we lead in drag.

Queerness is a deliberate way to challenge how we make ourselves known, how we present ourselves—as human beings, as people of God, as clergy. It invites me, as a unique, human being in this role to experiment with the physical boundaries around what is normative in the expression of this role. Queerness takes makeup, clothing, shoes, gestures, and voices and uses them as materials for play. It is a creative refashioning of gender and sexuality, much as my children will take markers to color their bodies so they are remade into purple tigers and green bears that growl and chase imaginary prey throughout the house. It is resistance, too, against those standards and expectations that try to squeeze people into certain molds, and it is a means for survival.

The first time I experienced the possibility of life abundant in this kind of resistance was at a drag show during a Pride celebration. This particular show had only drag queens, though drag kinging is more common now, particularly in university communities. Drag queens are men—both gay and straight—who perform in women's clothing, although they are not necessarily female impersonators. Drag kings include female-bodied individuals performing masculinity, transgender-identified performers performing masculinity or femininity, and female-identified individuals (known as "bio queens") performing femininity. Though there is a plethora of scholarship on drag queens, drag kinging is a relatively more recent phenomenon. Drag queens tend to engage in gender transition early in life and come to drag in part as a resolution of gender-identity issues. In contrast, drag kings tend to rethink their gender identities as a result of doing drag.

In "Drag Queens and Drag Kings: The Difference Gender

Makes,"[1] Leila J. Rupp, Verta Taylor, and Eve Ilana Shapiro researched two drag troupes, examining the very different ways that members of these troupes come to drag and the different kinds of theoretical and political consciousness they express. Yet despite the differences in their performances, drag queens and drag kings alike embody resistance to the gender structure and heteronormativity. "Both troupes use entertainment as a means of education, and both groups create solidarity among queer audience members."[2] Both troupes encourage viewers to see the ways that "consciously performed gender" plays with those rigid and binary categories around gender and sexuality. For example, some heterosexual men reported being surprisingly aroused at drag queen shows. Performing different genders in different ways, evoking a range of sexual identities, and eliciting nonnormative sexual desires from audience members, their performances have impact on their audiences by subverting expectations around presentation and connection.

Drag remakes how I wear the robe by expanding the boundaries around it, whether it is with hair down and bright red lipstick and high heels, or hair cropped short and no makeup, or hair tied back in a bun with huge earrings. There is no one way to wear it. It isn't solely male or female, masculine or feminine, yet just as one can be absent, both can be present simultaneously. Drag is a way to resist the narratives that constantly say gender is natural or neutral rather than a social construction mediated by cultural expectations. It provokes us to occupy limitless possibilities through play—for fun. A friend who is a gay Episcopal priest once joked with me that there's a reason why so many gay men are priests: the beautiful and dramatic vestments. It's the pageantry.

The clergy robe is drag. When we recognize the embodied conflict of the robe and present the role of clergy in more complex ways, then we communicate something about God, too. And we say something about the church.

Queerness means we expect the unexpected in what is presented and represented in the pulpit. Thinking about the difference gender makes in intentional performances of femininity and masculinity and the acting out of complex sexual desires can also help us to understand how enacting gender and sexuality in everyday life can challenge the gender and sexual system. In other words, drag can make us conscious, as well as conscientious, about how we perform, how we make intelligible, and how we make our bodies, our voices, and our work compelling and real.

Slaying the Binary

The first woman I saw preach in a pulpit was Nancy Lammers-Gross, a homiletics professor. It was during the opening convocation of my first semester in seminary. I was in awe of how comfortable she was in her robe up there in that massive pulpit, as if that pulpit were made just for her, as if she had spent all her life there. She had the entire chapel like putty in the palm of her hand. Everyone laughed riotously at the familiar angst in encountering New Jersey roads for the first time when she exclaimed indignantly, "You have to turn right to turn left!" (The way to make a standard left turn off Route 1 is to turn right onto something called a jug handle, which is a ramp on the right side of the road.) Hardly a dry eye was found at the end as she spoke effortlessly of God's grace in this baffling journey we were beginning in seminary. I thought, looking at her through grateful tears, *God willing, I am going to do that and be that someday.*

All new students took speech classes, where we had to practice reading Scripture passages out loud, in a compelling, dramatic fashion, which felt silly and forced at first, as if we were rehearsing lines for a play—learning when to pause, how to use dynamics, using gestures and moving our hands in a certain way, and practicing changing the tone and inflection in our voices. But as when my children play pretend, we discovered the miracle of learning through play, and we were able to experiment with the meaning of these biblical stories through all the ways we told them. Our teacher was so gentle and accommodating that I began to feel the power in my own voice. Even in its tremors and frequent squeakiness, I felt something that was true within me emerging for the world. In telling these stories in such an intentional way, we were embodying them, and it was a way of putting them on like outfits or costumes, but in such a way they became a part of us. There was little emphasis on the traditional expressions of the masculine or feminine, and anyone could perform any part in the dialogues in the Bible stories.

Speech was a prerequisite to Preaching 101 and 102, which involved a year of trying out the craft of writing and delivering sermons. It was completely different. My teacher was an older, white man who had an intimidating voice that transported you to a time when people listened to all the news on the radio. He had a rather narrow view of preaching. Not finding myself able to fit in that space around the pulpit, I began to shrivel up a bit and focused on passing the class. I lost confidence. I lost myself. It took many years into my ministry for that turmoil and misery I felt in the pulpit to disappear as I grew into my own mold, rather than trying to squeeze into a shape that was never meant to fit me.

I wonder how the pulpit—such an ordinary work of carpentry—became so entrenched in our world as a controversial object. One day, a long time ago, Andy remarked to me, as I was describing what I was learning in a Gender Studies class, more joking than serious, "The pulpit is kind of phallic, isn't it?" I grimaced at the thought, but then I was intrigued. The pulpit is a symbol of the patriarchy. Yet the more I think about who traditionally occupies that space and how they use it, I realize the subtle power of such a commodity.

Think of the many stories about abuses of the pulpit where male clergy spew judgment and all the ways people are dehumanized and experience violence because their pastors use the authority of the pulpit to manipulate people for their own benefit. There's the condemnation of "those homosexuals" (something I heard from a Presbyterian minister preaching on Romans when I was an impressionable college student), "abortion doctors" at Planned Parenthood, and "foreigners" (as when Muslims and Mexicans are ridiculed and oppressed from the "pulpit" held by our current US president). When you consider the histories of assault—verbal, emotional, psychological, spiritual, and theological—suddenly, references to principalities and powers take on a whole new meaning. And while most pastors in the pulpit may seem innocuous, we can't deny the subtle power of systems of US religion in which those who benignly preach about sin, injustice, and the world's evils are consistently those who look like the traditionally rich and powerful: white, male, and citizens.

Maybe the pulpit *is* phallic, in a way. I didn't necessarily feel penis envy, as in Freud's notion that females desire the phallus. I didn't desire the pulpit in that way, at least, not all the time. But I did feel acutely the unwelcome there—not just in the pulpit itself, but often in the pews. Like the clergy robe, it represented a space that could be occupied only by certain bodies, that is, usually white, male or masculine-presenting bodies. Power, authority, and legitimate calling were rooted in this very specific, narrow way, and despite my own ordination status, I struggled with the demons that whispered doubt about my ability or calling. It wasn't just the robe or the pulpit, but the words and the language of the liturgy, the songs, prayers, and references all around us, all the time. People still defaulted to the male and masculine without thinking when it came to speaking about God.

I've visited or been a regular participant in many churches across cultures and denominations, not just Presbyterian. The language of the liturgy is a major tell, especially the pronouns used when referencing God. Some communities depend on tradition and an "it's the way we've always done it" mentality, while others display a willingness to engage the current context with sensitivity. The subtle but powerful difference between singing the Doxology with the words "Praise him, all creatures here below" and "Praise God, all creatures here below" is not lost on me, and it's reinforced by the conversations I have with my six-year-old daughter, who unconsciously refers to God with the masculine pronoun. It's a reminder that there is much in the air all around us, and that what often becomes normalized isn't necessarily forced or coerced in aggressive ways. Sometimes it's just a three-letter word.

All of this is a small part of the many conversations around how we regulate gender, how we regulate who represents the church and, ultimately, the Divine. The quandary around gender is a bit of a chicken-or-egg kind of a question, even a nature-versus-nurture kind of conversation, which can sometimes feel futile. Powerful discourses and mechanisms produce our notions of the masculine and feminine, which are connected to gender identity. But queerness offers a way to use gender itself as a way to deconstruct such notions, as with drag troupes and as with clergy robes. We can play. We can perform. We can push the boundaries of presentation. We can actually use gender to move beyond the naturalized binary when we refer to "gender trouble" or "gender blending," "transgender," and more.[3] In the same way, the pulpit can be used as an instrument to dismantle the norms around masculinity and femininity associated with a specific gender.

In other words, we can use the pulpit to critique and challenge the norms that regulate it. A queer spirituality slays the binary.

Queering Vocation

I'm drawn to the Bible stories of women like Deborah, Ruth and Naomi, Esther, Mary, and Lydia, who stood in their own power. They each seemed to have their own kind of gravity and shifted the reality around them. But the story of the nameless woman—the one who shows up in two gospels in a handful of sentences barely worth mentioning—speaks to me more than anything else. In Matthew she is the Canaanite woman, and in Mark she is the Syrophoenician woman. In other words, she is a gentile, a foreigner and enemy, one who occupies the bottom rung. She was no better than a dog, or to use a colloquialism accurate to that time, a "little bitch," as Jesus himself calls her.

As these stories often go, we read that Jesus is tired and finds respite at an unknown home. Somehow this woman finds out and immediately goes to him. In the Matthew version, she begins shouting at him, calling him "Son of David," asking for mercy, and annoying the disciples, who ask that Jesus send her away. In both accounts, she positions herself at Jesus's feet and begs for his help for the sake of her daughter, who is possessed by a demon. Jesus attempts to deflect her request, mumbling something about only going to the lost sheep of the house of Israel. "It is not fair to take the children's food and throw it to the dogs" (Matthew 15:26). And then her response: "Yes, Lord, yet even the dogs eat the crumbs that fall from their masters' table" (Matthew 15:27).

What is going on with Jesus in this moment? Some scholars suggest that Jesus doesn't fully realize his mission is for all—Jew and gentile—until this moment. It takes an outsider woman to come to him and squarely place herself in front of him. Not only does this woman have the audacity to speak to Jesus in the first place, but she schools him. And in speaking truth to power, she shifts history. Jesus realizes that the kingdom is meant for all. The table is wide enough for every single human being.

Somehow this woman, likely deemed unclean and therefore despicable and expendable, recognizes Jesus. (In some ways, she recognizes him before his own disciples do.) She calls him "Son of David," a sign of his kingship, and in the custom of one addressing royalty, she kneels before him at his feet. There is a connection between those who kneel before Jesus and the healings that Jesus performs. A leper kneels before Jesus and asks to be made clean (Matthew 8:2). A ruler kneels and asks for his daughter's healing (9:18). At the end of this Gospel, when the resurrected Lord appears, the disciples bow before him, and Jesus says that all authority in heaven and earth is his (28:17-18).

What it reminds me is that power and authority aren't always just a matter of leadership or administration, but of occupying the space fully, honestly, and bravely, whether at the pulpit or beneath a table. The Canaanite woman doesn't deny who she is at the time, or her context, or the social-political realities all around her, but she also doesn't let these limit her perspective on what it means that Jesus is the Son of David. This woman kneels before one whom she recognizes as having authority, not only to sit on the throne of David, but also to wield power over evil. It's that courageous recognition that changes Jesus. Even Jesus can be changed.

If Jesus can be changed, then I can, too, and so can the church that I love. All around me, I see hope for the church poured out. I see it in campus ministry, working alongside a young lesbian couple who served as interns for a year and being inspired by their boundless enthusiasm for this community. I see the everyday dedication of a gay friend who is the rector of the downtown Episcopalian church. He shows me how to keep learning, asking, and caring for people in ways they just don't teach you in seminary. Hope abounds when I'm working with another lesbian couple on a project that is a monthly gathering of stories and song as a space for LGBTQIA people in our local context. There was the Sunday in the sanctuary of a moderate, mainline congregation where I enjoyed the heartwarming sight of being led in worship by a transwoman and one of the clergy members of the congregation who is gay and recently married. And there's a gay Latino PhD student in the gender studies program at Indiana University who loves people and sees incredible possibility in queering Jesus and what that means for him and his own social and activist work. These are snippets of story after story I encounter on a regular basis—stories of a wide range of people from all walks of life who live and love from their bodies, their desires, and their passions, and who shape the way I understand calling and vocation.

Vocation isn't limited to the pulpit, nor to the clergy and church workers, and certainly not to parish or any kind of formal Christian ministry. It is more than a job or occupation, more than employment, it is a calling. It is a way to grasp how we occupy space in this world—to delve into the question of what kind of work will be an expression and extension of our deepest selves. This is not about an understanding of labor critiqued by Marxists and anti-capitalists, but about the kind of work that is connected to who we are as the result of God's own loving labor. When work is tied to vocation, and when vocation is grounded in God's desire for our participation in something meaningful and life-giving, then all work is liturgical; it is an act of worship and glorying of God. For me, this has meant realizing that whether I live my days behind a pulpit or behind a teacher's or writer's desk or behind a kitchen counter or behind a coffee bar, I'm engaging my deepest longing by attending to the Spirit of God in that moment. And all these spaces offer the possibility of play—of connecting, listening, and learning more about God and more about humanity. Work becomes a way to reciprocate God's own faithful and passionate activity in the world, and anyone and everyone is invited into it. A queer spirituality leads me to see all the possible ways I occupy that space and make room for others, too, for all of us to fulfill our calling, that labor of love.

It is what I love about the Reformed perspective of the

priesthood of all believers, because it revolutionizes how we understand each person's place specifically in the body of Christ; that is, all are tasked with bringing the good news to bear in all places. But it means more than the promise of each person's vocation tied to Christ's body. It also encompasses the beauty and power of every person's flesh-and-blood body as an expression of God's very kingdom. Sometimes that's the same "job" for fifty years. Sometimes it's cobbling together numerous side projects. Sometimes it brings in an income. Sometimes it means taking out student loans. Whatever that vocation looks like in whatever scenario, it's a different way to express that faithfulness to bodies (other lives around you) and to being embodied, created, and an expression of God's own vocation in creation, redemption, and transformation.

Even as I continue in this unmoored way to struggle with my identity and what it means to be queer in this work, I need the community and the stories to show me the way. I am able to move past and through all my qualms by occupying, experimenting, and problematizing what my calling means. This is queering vocation. The waters of baptism are deep and wide, and we are meant to swim and play like children on the first day of summer vacation. A queer spirituality recognizes that these joyous and hopeful waters not only transform each individual, their hopes, their aspirations, and their work; they also transform the shape and life of the entire body of Christ.

Notes

1. Leila J. Rupp, Verta Taylor, and Eve Ilana Shapiro, "Drag Queens and Drag Kings: The Difference Gender Makes," *Sexualities* 13, no. 3 (2010): 275–294.
2. Rupp, Taylor, and Shapiro, "Drag Queens and Drag Kings," 290.
3. Butler, *Undoing Gender* (New York: Routledge, 2004), 42.

9

Purity Culture and the Christian Wrong

Blessed are the pure in heart, for they shall see God.
—Matthew 5:8

Right before my freshman year in high school, my parents and I moved into a house on the north side of my hometown of Colorado Springs. A friend invited me to attend her church, and I did for much of high school. The church had charismatic youth-group gatherings, home Bible studies, and special services, like the one on Good Friday, which came complete with an altar call. I slid into these experiences, mimicking speaking in tongues and trying to move my hands and body the same way during worship. There was something comforting and familiar. Perhaps the more emotional expression of faith reminded me of my own family's church.

But after a while, it felt forced and exhausting, and I found myself with my eyes open most of the time, looking around during the prayers at those dancing and singing. I was suddenly more interested in what this faith looked like and less in what it felt like. I stopped attending as much and eventually quit altogether.

My friend's church was called New Life Church. Maybe you've heard of it.

Long after I graduated from seminary, I came across a headline about this church, which became one of the most influential Christian organizations in the United States. The church was caught in a shocking scandal that sent crippling reverberations throughout the evangelical Christian world. The senior pastor of the church, Ted Haggard, faced allegations of an extramarital affair. He had bought drugs and solicited a male sex worker in Denver for over three years. According to CNN, "After the allegations were made public, Haggard resigned as president of the influential National Association of Evangelicals (NAE), an umbrella group representing more than 45,000 churches with 30 million members. He also temporarily stepped aside as pastor of the 14,000-member New Life Church."[1]

Eventually, the church board forced Haggard to completely resign and pushed his family out. But for the wider evangelical Christian community, the target of criticism became the "homosexual act" Haggard had committed. The rhetoric suggested that his misconduct was much more offensive than if he'd had an affair with a heterosexual woman. And those who were virulently opposed to homosexuality weren't solely evangelical Christians. Arguably, this perspective was held widely by those who fall on the conservative side of the political spectrum.

It was no coincidence that "Christian" and "Right" were often synonymous, and sadly, in the public sphere, it continues to be so today. Early forces included renowned evangelist Billy Graham, who supported Republican candidates and had a huge hand in forming a religious Republican base through his revivalist campaigns, and the cross-denominational organizing of the National Evangelicals Association. As the influence of evangelical Christianity in politics stretched all the way up to the Oval Office, the Christian Right became more than just a political perspective or single organization.

What happened with Haggard was an issue of morality and fidelity, and the betrayal of heterosexuality. Ultimately, it was an issue of purity, and it betrayed all the structures around virginity. In our church and society, we have a culture of purity, which regulates bodies and locks people into narrow, limited sexualities.

I barely remember Ted Haggard, but I doubt I will ever forget this story; it arouses so many emotions, including sadness, outrage, shock, relief, and doubt. The story is a part of the history of the town where I grew up, as well as of American Christianity, my faith, and our American notions of purity and faithfulness. The effects of purity culture are still present in the dogmatism of purity balls and rings, increasing controversies over wedding cakes for gay couples, and gender-specific signage for public restrooms.

But this is not the only Christian way to view purity. A few days ago, I received a postcard from the group Queer Theology, and on the front it says, "Christianity has always been queer." It was a timely reminder that Christianity has actually always contended with notions of purity through queerness. From its beginnings, Christianity was characterized by transgressive encounters, the crossing of boundaries—an offensive intermingling, whether it involves temple meat or worship, multiple ethnicities and identities, and friendships that extend beyond the norm. A queer spirituality today continues that legacy by challenging and dismantling the kind of purity that locks people out, locks people in their bodies, or locks people out of the fullest expression of faithfulness we are called to and created for in God. A queer spirituality says, "To hell with your purity," because purity doesn't define love or value, no matter how pretty and shiny you make it. Purity doesn't define or indicate faith or faithfulness or the nature of God's covenant with us. Purity doesn't define goodness or holiness, and it isn't a measure of salvation.

Like a Virgin

But people sure do try to make purity everything—pretty and shiny, good and holy, and faithful to God. We have not only a culture of purity but a cult of purity, where virginity is glorified and exalted. The return to conservatism in the 1980s began a resurgence of interest in womanly purity and "biblical" gender roles. With the set roles of the 1950s facing upheaval, many conservative evangelicals scrambled for a foothold, and some found it in fairy-tale-like methods for promoting virginity, especially of their daughters.

When I was getting ready to graduate from high school, my parents gave me a ring with a pearl to wear on my left hand. They said something along the lines of "promising myself to God" and "being pure and faithful," obviously thinking about college and all the stories of what happens to most normal, red-blooded teenagers when you cram thousands of them together in a small space. There wasn't anything overtly ceremonial or formal about this moment, but it stayed with me, even after I failed to keep the promise my freshman year in college by sleeping with my boyfriend at the time. I still kept the ring, but I didn't wear it. I struggled with trying to reconcile "giving up" my virginity with my continued love of and faith in God. No one in my Christian communities addressed these struggles, except those who talked about a second or renewed virginity, though the groups that were "gracious" enough to create a language where people could sexually "start over" still centered the necessity of purity and always couched it in a language of holiness and faith.

This obsession with virginity—specifically, chastity and abstinence—wasn't necessarily about preventing STDs or teenage pregnancies. It seemed hypothetical in many ways. There were parental gifts of a "purity ring" in exchange for a pledge of sexual abstinence, and some communities even held "purity balls." Purity balls actually began in Colorado Springs. They were, and still are, debutante-style, coming-of-age parties for mostly adolescent daughters. Young girls in fancy ballroom dresses attended a special dance, escorted by their fathers. Featured at the ball were a cross, white flowers, and a military-style Arch of the Saber ceremony. Vows were spoken, and contracts signed. In *The Virgin Tales,* a documentary on purity balls, Swiss producer Mirjam von Arx focuses on the Wilson family and their organization, Generations of Light, which began hosting purity balls at the Broadmoor Hotel in 1998. Participants take this concept of purity of body and mind one step further, declaring that even their first kiss would be at the altar. According to a summary description of the documentary, "For two years, the filmmakers follow the Wilson offspring as they prepare for their fairytale vision of romance and marriage and seek out their own prince and princess spouses. In the process, a broader theme emerges: how the religious right is grooming a young generation of virgins to embody an Evangelically-grounded Utopia in America."[2]

At its peak, dozens of these events were held all over the United States, sponsored by churches and other Christian nonprofit groups. Writes Jennifer Baumgardner in a 2007 article in *Glamour* magazine, "The balls embody one of [evangelical Christianity's] key doctrines: abstinence until marriage. Thousands of girls have taken purity vows at these events over the past nine years."[3] Purity—specifically, chastity—became chic in a way.

The popularity of purity balls showed that the cult of virginity was becoming a fast-growing movement, but many iterations of the concept had already been in place. True Love Waits (sponsored by LifeWay), Acquire the Fire (Teen Mania Ministries), and Silver Ring Thing were hosting gatherings that resembled a combination of a rave, a *Saturday Night Live* show, and a Sunday-night revival.

At the same time, the promotion of purity isn't found in just Christian circles, such as youth ministries, campus ministries, and other faith organizations. In her book *The Purity Myth,* Jessica Valenti explains that purity culture extends beyond these federally funded dances. These days, Facebook is peppered with purity groups that exist to support girls trying to "save it." Schools hold abstinence rallies and assemblies featuring hip-hop dancers and comedians alongside religious leaders. Disturbingly, but maybe not surprising, with the current rise of evangelicalism in the broader culture and politics, Valenti observes that "virginity and chastity are reemerging as a trend in pop culture, in our schools, in the media, and even in legislation. Young women are . . . simultaneously being taught that their only real worth is their virginity and ability to remain pure."[4]

The theatrical frame of the purity ball gives meaning to the daughter's virginity by elevating it. Given the way that fathers, daughters, and also mothers solidify distinct ideologies around virginity by lifting it up and *worshipping* it, I was expecting a purity chant or anthem to go along with the whole phenomenon, if there wasn't one already. In essence, the daughter's virginity is primary and, in many ways, a separate entity from her.

A closer look at purity balls reveals a pervasive culture that reinforces more than a sexual morality or ideal. And while these dances weren't exactly on my radar when I was a teenager, this culture of pledging my virginity to God was absolutely real for me, too. Virginity was tied to salvation. But purity wasn't just a matter of salvation or faith; it also was and is about worth, about value. And it made the wheels of society turn. Without it, heteropatriarchy would have no power.

Jessica Valenti says, "The lie of virginity—the idea that such a thing even exists—is ensuring that young women's perception of themselves is inextricable from their bodies, and that their ability to be moral actors is absolutely dependent on their sexuality."[5] Virginity as the measure of a person's (especially a woman's) morality means that nothing else matters—not what women accomplish, not what women think, not what women care about and work for. All that matters is if and how women have sex, and with whom. That's all.

Though purity balls are less common now, the idea that virginity and purity are synonymous remains. This is true even beyond the culture of American Protestantism or evangelicalism. It's undeniable how present it is everywhere.

Keep It Clean, Keep It Bright

Purity culture is woven into the fabric of everyday life so much so that when we are confronted with it in everyday images on buses, magazines, or commercials for Hulu, people hardly bat an eye. Early in the summer of 2017, the skin-care brand Nivea pulled an ad that depicted a woman in white in a bright room with the words, "Keep it clean, keep it bright. Don't let anything ruin it," and "White is purity." Soon people correctly called out the ad, with one blogger describing it as "something that looks like it'd be on the front desk of Hitler's spa."[6] The company apologized in an official statement: "We are deeply sorry to anyone who may take offense to this specific post. Diversity and equal opportunity are crucial values of Nivea."[7]

Purity culture subordinates women's bodies but goes even further by necessarily devaluing dark skin, in essence, to erase nonwhite bodies. Christianity is used as an instrument of systems of power to regulate bodies through the insidious tenets of purity culture. Through the force of religion, the cultures and systems of purity seek to control any bodies that would threaten the concept of purity—especially black and brown bodies and the bodies of those whose sexual identities are deemed unintelligible or reprehensible according to institutional powers, whether it's the nation-state or the church, schools or the courtroom.

The values that drive the decisions, perspectives, and ultimately the beliefs of the religious go beyond bodies. These values aren't necessarily abstract but are associated with God, with eternity, "out there." This makes them more real, more vital, more urgent, so that even wedding cakes and restrooms are contested by those who hold these values. Purity is routinely cultivated—through rituals and practices, and even through normal, everyday life—with notions of cleanliness and whiteness. Purity as whiteness is so normalized that even something like the ad copy for a brand of soap seems routine and innocent.

Those who hold these purity values constantly push beyond the embodied and material life for absolute answers by devaluing humanity and belittling all its wonderful complexities. Purity relies on hierarchies in systems of power and privilege, of dominance and subjugation, where one or some are "on high" or "above" or "beyond." Of course, this means the rest are subject to the one who is transcendent. Women are subject to men; LGBTQIA persons are subject to cisgender heterosexual persons; people of color are subject to those who are white.

Purity is about power and dominance, according to theologian Mark Taylor: "In the history of dominant Christian thinking, the examples of this are many: God is privileged over world then heaven over earth, spirit over matter, the pure over impure, white over nonwhite, man over woman, heterosexual over trans-sexual persons. . . . A key example is Christianity's centuries of linking whiteness and purity to its sovereign God, a figure which had to be stripped of its material impurities, kept in a *pure white* beyond" (emphasis mine).[8]

For a long time, my nonwhiteness felt like queerness, even though I only recently named it as such. I felt abnormal, other, strange, and lesser. I was surrounded by whiteness for a majority of my waking life and tried to avoid noticing it. I hated feeling not normal, and it was exacerbated whenever I felt my foreignness and was reminded of that queerness. I wasn't clean and bright. I wasn't white—just one more condition added to the list that made me lacking. Not white, not male, not straight, not a virgin. Therefore, not Christian enough, or just not really Christian. At best, I felt myself a second-class human.

Purity isn't just about sex or sexuality, or about gender identity and gender roles; it's always about race and ethnicity, nationality, ability, and more. To define itself, it needs the Other. It needs those binaries of black or white, colonizer or colonized, father or daughter, male or female, chaste or defiled. These categories are necessary for purity to be useful as an instrument that propagates a certain system that gives power to some.

There are stories that complicate all these intersections. One such example is the story of the pioneering transsexual woman Christine Jorgenson. She was a transwoman who, after service in the US Army, became the first American to undergo sex-reassignment surgery. She introduced the American public to a new gender identity—transsexuality—in a way that didn't threaten the "natural" order. She was a blond beauty and domestically inclined, as well as the embodiment of middle-class values, and this made her acceptable. She demonstrated an idealized femininity. And she became quite popular as a result, finding herself on the cover of the *New York Daily News* and the *American Daily*. Perhaps unsurprisingly, "it was those transwomen . . . depicted with the most proximity to white womanhood, who gained the most visibility in the mainstream press and whose stories therefore came to define the boundaries of transsexual identity."[9]

Yet, no matter how positively Jorgenson was presented for public consumption by the media, I cannot imagine that living into her identity as transgender during that time period was easy. And then she was also used to shore up the boundaries of ethnosexual frontiers, so that especially transwomen of color were further alienated because they did not fit the gender norms or whiteness of purity culture. Purity isn't black and white, but if history tells us anything, it prefers whiteness.

The virgin daughters at purity balls are caught in a similar system of oppression and coercion. Despite all their economic and social status, they are victims of the patriarchal institutions of family and religion. The only benefits they glean from their enculturation in this system are institutional approval and protection from the consequences, as long as they don't break the rules of this system. They are passive participants with little voice or agency. Their bodies are used to perpetuate certain identities and sexualities—white, heterosexual, and Christian—which are privileged but lifeless outside of purity. These balls, then, are not just father-daughter dances.

But whether we're thinking of purity balls or commercials for soap or razors, all of these rituals, images, objects, and systems of power and privilege sacralize purity. Purity is made sacred through virginity, through ethnicity, through sexual and gender identity, and it solidifies the compulsory nature of heterosexual relationships. Even today, though the products and stories are a little different, the force of these religious and cultural ideals is in the power of the ritual, whether it's putting on a fake silver ring, signing a pledge, or saying "I do" to your father and committing your virginity to him.

Not only is seeing believing, but doing is believing, too. At the level of seeing pictures of white Jesus and in the subliminal messaging that "white is pure," these acts and messages cultivate belief in purity, in the sanctifying power of purity. The worship of the pure ideal is made even more tangible in these practices and performances. Purity is inscribed on white bodies, and the opposite on nonwhite bodies. But a queer spirituality resists these systems, and it interrogates the existence of purity as morality and purity as identity. A queer spirituality creates the possibility of a new kind of faithfulness that is oriented away from the center of power and privilege.

Queering Faithfulness

I tried to be pure. I tried to behave and to do all the right things, because I thought belief would materialize if I went through the motions. I thought I could fulfill the expectations of what it meant to be a woman of faith—a pure woman, a faithful woman. But the more I tried to do, the less I believed, because what was on the outside didn't match up with what was happening on the inside. I wasn't seeing the same ideals and images of purity in myself. I didn't feel I was seen in the same way. As much as I tried to be, feel, and sound "faithful" (by the standards of the white, suburban Christians around me), I carried the shame of my original sin: giving up my virginity. I felt I had to resign myself—and my future husband, God, and my family—to a lesser, illegitimate faithfulness. I would never achieve the kind of faithfulness God wanted of me, because I had sullied myself on so many levels. My faithfulness could only go so far. And it meant my faith could only go so far, too. It cloaked me in a shame I didn't release until I stopped believing that virginity and whiteness—in other words, purity—constitute the only formula for salvation.

There wasn't any lightning-strike moment, like a Saul-to-Paul conversion on the road. There was nothing like what that adulterous woman might have experienced when she was made to stand in front of Jesus in the temple, only to be released and sent on her way. The Gospel of John (8:1-11) is the only place where this story is told: a woman who was caught (in bed? making breakfast in the kitchen of her lover? in the shower after the act?) was mercilessly hauled out by the scribes and Pharisees to receive judgment according to the law of Moses.

For a long time, when I read this story, in good Reformed fashion, I focused only on Jesus. I observed how he was in the middle of teaching the people, how he must have felt tired from the constant interruptions from those trying to catch him in the act of breaking Moses's commands. *They're back at it again?* I noted how Jesus heard the demands of his critics and saw this woman standing in front of him, chin pointed down, hair and clothes disheveled, maybe even without shoes. I thought about Jesus bending down from his chair and scribbling something in the sand. (How many Sunday school and youth group activities have I done where we were to imagine and draw what Jesus drew in the sand?) I pondered how he stood up and spoke his truth, and no one could respond in any other way but by dropping one stone after another on the ground and walking away.

But this story isn't just about Jesus—or just about the woman. It's about both of them: "Jesus was left alone with the woman standing before him. Jesus straightened up and said to her, 'Woman, where are they? Has no one condemned you?' She said, 'No one, sir.' And Jesus said, 'Neither do I condemn you. Go your way, and from now on do not sin again," (John 8: 9b-11). Maybe now she stood in front of him with her head held high, even defiant and unashamed.

This isn't the forgiveness of sins we see Jesus offer in other miracles. *He simply doesn't condemn her.*

I'm back to the Ted Haggard story. For me, purity isn't just about holiness—a moral chasteness and stale perfection. It's also about faithfulness. The people who demand purity want to control holiness and faithfulness, and in essence, they want to control people—their bodies, their souls. This is wrong. It's simply, totally wrong. I was sad for Haggard, confused and absorbed by the stories of his life after New Life. Jeff Chu, author of *Does Jesus Really Love Me?*, had a chance to interview Haggard many years later. At this point, Haggard is back in Colorado Springs and has started a new church; his wife has a couple of best-selling books, including *Why*

I Stayed; and his children are mostly grown and scattered around the country.

He doesn't hide or cower behind the pain or the shame, but neither does he deny it. He also doesn't care what others think in terms of image control or damage control—whether people think he's gay, bi, or straight. All he cares about is resurrection and redemption, and he pursues them obsessively, relentlessly. You can read it in his words. "Nobody is perfect. But no matter what, you can be okay. You don't have to live in shame. You don't have to go through the worst experience of your life and let that define you."[10] Haggard is not bound by shame. He's not defined by the misconduct of his past. He's not carrying on as a condemned soul. He's fully aware that he needs Christ and that we all need Christ. Despite the huge fall from grace, he hasn't given up on Jesus or the message of Jesus. To me, that's faithfulness. And it's so strange and queer, and though I don't totally agree with it or get his view, I find myself compelled by his willingness to choose life.

The woman who was caught in the act of adultery didn't receive judgment, condemnation, or death, even though all of these would be well within the rights of the community. After all, the laws were there to help the people uphold purity, and Jesus knew that. The religious leaders were aware of it. The people expected it. But the value of a human being is love, not morality, not virginity, and not whiteness or proximity to whiteness. We want so desperately for there to be black-and-white answers (actually, just white answers)—clear, clean, and undeniable words and laws written in ink on sacred scrolls. But sometimes faithfulness is scribbled into the dirt, and then wiped away. Answers cleared away like the chaff with the wind, a moment that doesn't define a whole person's life but is sometimes the key that unlocks our redemption.

***

Even though I no longer view purity as the path to redemption, I still struggle with feelings of shame over the loss of my perceived purity in college. But this shame is complicated by the trauma of sexual assault I experienced after I graduated from college and lived in a small town in upstate New York. When I think back to that night during the summer of 2000, though I don't have physical proof or evidence of it, I know deep in my bones I did not drink enough to black out at a house party. I was friends with most of the guys there; in fact, I was casually dating one of them. But that night I was chatting it up with one of his roommates. Except after a few drinks, the walls got fuzzy with the light undulating and fading, and I started to see black spots. It crossed my mind, briefly: *He slipped something into my drink.* I was alarmed and knew I needed to get home. I remember this clearly—saying *no,* stumbling to his door trying to leave his bedroom. But he shut it methodically, firmly and stood in front of it, and I said again, "No, no, no," and then the world went dark.

I still feel responsible. I still feel like it was my fault. I still feel dirty, morally reprehensible, and like I deserved to wake up the next morning completely naked next to someone who was basically a stranger. I was confused and disoriented, ashamed and lost, thinking, "Maybe I encouraged him."

No. That was wrong.

Some years later, when I was in seminary, I attended a service of healing for those who have dealt with sexual assault and violence. The moment I stood up to light a candle for myself, for others I knew in my life, and for my companions in the chapel, I felt that light break through. It caused a little crack in the layers and layers I had piled up around that moment. Some of that light is painful, remembering and reliving it, but I need to see it over and over for its lies about my body and humanity. I've found that each time I confront it, acknowledge it, share it, and speak it out aloud as a part of my history, as part of my participation in history alongside other people who have experienced the same, I let in more of this light, it diminishes the darkness and corruption to my soul and agency, and I can face a little more head-on anything that would repudiate my humanity, my belovedness, and my redemption.

Redemption is for all, for the sake of living and loving. A queer spirituality sheds light on all the ways the powers-that-be bind us up in shame and pain, and on the ways those lines are tangled up with race, gender, sexuality, ability, and generation. Purity is insidious this way. It pretends that the categories are clear-cut, but it relies on the ways identity is full of paradoxes and contradictions. Purity isn't limited to Christianity, or to evangelical Christianity, or even to American evangelicalism. It's a powerful global force found in cultures and religions thousands of years old. What's unique about American evangelicalism is the way purity is commodified, monopolized, packaged, and sold. It's also guarded and preserved and somehow untouched even by the worst stories of scandals and sexual assault committed by church leaders, lawmakers, and even the president of the United States.

Our value, our worth doesn't lie in the abstract or ideal of virginity. And purity isn't love. Morality isn't love. Holiness isn't love. Love is love. And every human being is worthy of it, of dignity, of agency, of grace.

Notes

1. Delia Gallagher, "Church Forces Out Haggard for 'Sexually Immoral Conduct,'" CNN, November 3, 2006, https:// tinyurl.com/ y8q6hx8m.

2. "WFF (2012) - Virgin Tales - Documentary Movie HD," YouTube video, 1:39, uploaded by "Movieclips Film Festivals & Indie Films," October 4, 2012, "show more" description, https://tinyurl.com/ y9qqa3wd.

3. Jennifer Baumgardner, "Would You Pledge Your Virginity to Your Father?," *Glamour*, January 1, 2007, https://tinyurl.com/y8paqd7u.

4. Jessica Valenti, *The Purity Myth* (Berkeley, CA: Seal, 2009), 9.

5. Valenti, *Purity Myth*, 9.

6. Joanna Rothkopf, "Nivea Pulls 'White Is Purity' Ad, But I'll Never Forget It," *Jezebel*, April 6, 2017, https://tinyurl.com/y8vwvp9f.

7. Rothkopf, "Nivea Pulls 'White Is Pruity' Ad."

8. Mark Lewis Taylor, "Christianity and US Prison Abolition: Rupturing a Hegemonic Christian Ideology," *Socialism and Democracy* 28, no. 3 (2014): 172–88, https://tinyurl.com/y7kzp2xf.

9. Emily Skidmore, "Constructing the 'Good Transsexual': Christine Jorgensen, Whiteness, and Heteronormativity in the Mid-

Twentieth-Century Press," *Feminist Studies* 37, no. 2 (Summer 2011): 271.

10. Jeff Chu, *Does Jesus Really Love Me? A Gay Christian's Pilgrimage in Search of God In America* (New York: Harper, 2013), 164.

10

Church Outside the Closet

Imagine if every church became a place where everyone is safe, but no one is comfortable. Imagine if every church became a place where we told one another the truth. We might just create sanctuary.

—Rachel Held Evans, *Searching for Sunday: Loving, Leaving, and Finding the Church*

"I didn't make it to church this morning."

This was something I have said quite a bit—and not just in college, when every Saturday night I was up too late for no good reason (though once in a while for a relatively good reason). I said it the most after we had children and moved to Bloomington. Regularly. Habitually. Each Sunday, I would wake up with so very many good intentions. The night before, as I drifted off to sleep, plans for the morning would have flitted through my mind: wake up before anyone else gets up, to squeeze in a shower and smell nice; make sure the babies eat breakfast and take a nap before church; clean the kitchen and start lunch.

I know, I know, the road to hell. . . . Anyway, I excelled at dreaming up plans like this for the babies. It turns out that that road is really soft and quiet, actually, and it beckons to me in the form of a couch and the warm sun streaming in from the window next to it. The babies went down for their nap. And so did I.

I was overcome with guilt. As a disciple of Jesus, then a pastor, and now a mother, responsible for the soul care of these babies, how could I miss church? (I know, I'm being overly dramatic.)

I struggled, and still do sometimes—with so many others, not only parents, but people in many walks and seasons of life—with how and what it means to be a part of church, the body of Christ, the beloved community, in loving relationship with God and others. For some, the struggle with church was not a choice, and I recognize the ways that many are shut out for reasons around their gender and sexuality. I've felt that same rejection, too.

For me, however, the struggle was not only about conforming in a certain way to fit in on Sunday mornings but also about what it means to walk the walk and talk the talk in all aspects of life. I've tended to think that my connection to God needed to be enacted in a certain way, like a checklist: church, Bible studies, choir practice, Sunday school, quiet times. But then I read a blog post from Penny Carothers that challenged this sense of obligation and offered the possibility of "the sanctification of the ordinary":

[Medievalist scholar Elizabeth Dreyer's idea that parenting is fertile ground for spirituality] has got me thinking: what if there really is a different way? What if God intended the hug of a child to mirror the numinous moment others achieve through meditation? What if attending to the needs and the play of children—really attending, not reading the news on my phone or folding laundry while I listen with half an ear—was a window into the spiritual? What if all I really needed to do was simply be present? After all, God calls himself a lover and a parent, and perhaps there is something to learn in embracing my life rather than trying to escape it so I can have *real* communion with God.[1]

This changed my life. It's still a little shocking to me, even today, that perhaps the most spiritual, even worshipful thing I can do is embrace my life as a mother. And I don't mean a platonically ideal mother, but a snot-wiping, baby-chasing, diaper-bag-toting mother, embracing the ordinary and everyday as a sacred act. Because our faith and identity aren't cultivated only by formal Bible studies, centering prayer, or the *lectio divina* (a traditional Benedictine way to read, pray, and meditate on Scripture slowly and intentionally), though these are good and wonderful. Rather, sometimes it's the simple "help!" and "thank you" that build any relationship, whether with God or with children or spouse. It's that simple.

All this meant that I didn't feel pressure to drag the twins and myself to church if it just didn't work out, and it would be all right. Lightning would not strike us from above. So most Sundays, we'd stay home, in our pajamas, and I tried to put on some classical music for a little bit. The babies and I listened to their Pap's sermons from previous Sundays on my iPhone. We banged rattles and cars. I sang "Spirit of the Living God" to them. We got out all the kitchen paraphernalia. I threw them up in the air a few times, just to hear them squeal and laugh. I played some hymns on the piano. We had crackers and juice, and then we ate lunch.

It felt good, but in the end, it wasn't church—not exactly. Though I felt moved and loved in the moment, and there was something inexpressibly spiritual happening those mornings, I was missing something. There simply is no substitute for gathering with the communion of saints each week, even if it doesn't look like traditional church or the church of my childhood. In fact, many Christian communities do life together in unconventional ways. For example, there are the intentional Catholic Worker groups, where families buy a cluster of homes and truly share life together with weekly meals, meetings, and extending hospitality to the neighborhood, especially those in need. Some churches meet in coffee houses, movie theaters, community gardens, and bars. Some take a complete Sabbath at least one Sunday a month and worship on Saturdays, or they meet during the week or once a month, or online, or in video chats. All these out-of-the-box expressions of church demonstrate both that the core of church is *ekklesia* being constantly called out, and that we also need to be called in, called to community, to be among our people regularly.

People do church today in ways that are less and less distinct from "secular" culture—that is, the rest of society, the stuff of the ordinary, everyday, mundane, regular spaces, actions, and gestures that fill our lives. The challenge is to carve out numerous spaces that allow for all these expressions of church—whether it's Sunday mornings at home with a podcast and piano, Thursday-night potlucks and a hymn sing, or sharing in the Eucharist at a dinner church service on a Sunday evening with a group of rowdy college students.

While it's hard for me not to think of church as only what happens on Sundays, specifically worship, I wonder if we've closeted the potential for living out that belovedness God intended not only for the body of Christ but for the whole human community at large. By lifting up the importance and necessity of church, we've constrained and forgotten how we are called to live in our neighborhoods day in and day out, in relationship with all the categories of people in our lives—acquaintances, strangers, colleagues, peers, and friends.

A queer spirituality dissolves those boundaries, and queering church means throwing open those doors and breaking down those walls, especially when it comes to participating in community life—the way we gather together, the way we worship, the spaces we find ourselves in. Queering church means queering our faith lives, too, and those boundaries and legalistic expectations to check off the religious to-do list. Queerness opens us to a more thoughtful and meaningful perspective, a willingness to see the possibility in what is different: all the different seasons and struggles, abilities, multiplicities, and convictions of each individual. There isn't one way to show up. And when we do show up, we don't have to be functioning at the same level or pitch. There's room for everyone's needs. There's room for everyone's gifts.

There's room for everyone's spiritual practices. There's room for everyone's visions. There's room for everyone's doubt. There's room for everyone's complexities. There's room for everyone.

Church for Everyone

> The church and the whorehouse arrived in the Far West simultaneously. And each would have been horrified to think it was a different facet of the same thing. But surely they were both intended to accomplish the same thing: the singing, the devotion, the poetry of the churches took a man out of his bleakness for a time, and so did the brothels.
>
> —John Steinbeck, *East of Eden*[2]

On the way home from an out-of-town meeting, I was sitting in the waiting area to board my next flight, staring out the huge windows. Airplanes inched along the ground and floated in the sky. My cloudy eyes turned to the TV screens on every wall around me, broadcasting *Good Morning America*, Fox News, and ESPN. The sight of a tabbed collar on one show caught my eye, so I squinted to read the yellow rectangle at the bottom, where it said, "Drive-Thru Church." A priest wearing an orange vest was standing in a parking lot, hunched over the open window of a car. He shook the driver's hand, and the car moved forward as another moved up.

Father Matthew is the priest I saw blessing people in their cars. He said, "We're trying to think outside of the box," and "quantity matters and not quality," and it's about "convenience." At that moment, I took these statements almost as insults. It was personal. Never would I say that "quantity matters" or that anyone should do churchy things out of "convenience." I slid down a little into my seat, afraid that the word *Christian* or *clergy* was somehow visibly tattooed on my forehead and everyone was looking at it. I despaired a little at this "whatever works" way of doing church. I remember thinking, "How does this inspire transformation?"

Where are the spiritual practices or disciplines present in Father Matthew's "drive-thru church," if they are at all?

Yet a queer spirituality breaks through even these borders, through any boundaries that mark out what's safe or what's real, that cut people off, that prevent people from connecting to something deeper. For many years, I've thought about the church as diaspora, a community of people scattered from heaven, creating pockets of communities migrating through this world together, knowing and believing their ultimate citizenship is eternal. Church is kind of a "borderland," as Gloria E. Anzaldúa writes: "It is in a constant state of transition. The prohibited and forbidden are its inhabitants."[3] When I read her words, I think about how much Jesus crossed over into what is prohibited and forbidden in his ministry, in all his dining, traveling, consorting, working, living, drinking, and partying with those who would fit that category of banned. And every time he crossed over, he created community by making space for everyone.

Yet our communities and these spaces are not without struggle. There's a struggle for lines to mark one's home or yard or walls or room, so that who you are makes sense. There's a struggle for love. The struggle is what binds us together, and we perform and embody it through words, sacrament and song, pews and prayers, cup and communion. It's how we resist the darkness. This is church. This is church for everyone.

I'm back to thinking about the drive-through church. In the report I saw, one congregant talked to the news reporter about the ways this interaction with the priest on her way to work actually made the experience of church more personal. I still couldn't help but think, "A three-minute Hail Mary or Our Father is *personal*?" I look at this woman in a minivan rushing about on a day that's likely full of errands and soccer practice and music lessons and post-office trips, and I breathe out to myself, "I have no right to judge what she needs from the church." But the pastor in me wonders and worries, like a mother hen, whether this is truly enough. Does it give her something beyond words? Does it feed her? Does it give her hope? Does it sustain her life? Does it point her to the Divine? Does it give her a glimpse of the peaceable kingdom? If the answer is yes, then that's church, too.

Maybe, actually *I* would say yes, because I'm that mom, the student, the pastor, the writer in the minivan rushing to finish the to-do list, and it's raining, and the car needs an oil change, and I have to start laundry and dinner, and return the books to the library. In that moment, in that slight touch, in that brief, automatic whirr of a window that goes down and back up again, maybe, yes, this woman in the minivan that looks like mine found her borderland, a place to find air in the in-between of life interrupted and chaos. Maybe she received peace in that handshake, in the breath that finally comes out after being held all day long to hold everything together, in the words spoken over and through her. Maybe her experience was something truly personal, something real, something that saved her.

Whether it's a bar or a brothel or a church or a parking lot, queerness widens those boundaries so that church is truly for everyone, so that it becomes a place of hospitality and solidarity, of connection, of radical grace, of glorifying God through our communion together. I think often of Nadia Bolz-Weber's words: "Yoga classes are great, but they're not bringing you a casserole when you get sick." It's in the unique space of church rooted in the radical love and grace of God that we can cultivate practices of wholeness and belovedness.

Queering Practices of Belovedness

I grew up hearing that church was the place where you could come with everything—all your baggage. Yet it often felt as if we still needed to check certain bags at the threshold, or in church-speak, in the narthex. Anything negative or not pretty and shiny had to be sequestered, shut away, closeted. The unspoken message was "Don't bring your sadness, doubts, criticism, hopelessness, angst, frustrations (unless it's about the coffee or homeless people on the corner), and certainly not your anger." Anger was the worst; it was the antithesis to any kind of social decorum, niceness, politeness, or respectability. Anger meant a lack of self-control and an excess of emotion, both of which were wholly undesirable.

But I discovered I was angry. I couldn't help it. All the time, I was angry at the world, angry at my (lack of) parenting skills, angry at how little time there was to think or reflect or write anything meaningful, angry at racism, angry at the church, angry at scarcity and shame, angry at the copious amount of dandelions peppering our lawn (one more thing on the to-do list for this suburban life), angry at sexism, angry at bigotry and prejudice, angry at violence and oppression, angry at extrajudicial killings of innocent black bodies, and angry at my exhaustion. In many ways, I'm still angry.

Since the twins were nine months old, I've been on a generic form of Zoloft for postpartum depression. The dosage is much less these days, since diet and some exercise, the occasional sleep, lunch with girlfriends, and massages help a great deal. Depression is still there, though, like an undercurrent, a discordant melody slightly coloring everything I see and feel. I suppose it is one of those realities that will remain in my life for a while. I tried going off medication for about eleven months and noticed a marked difference. I've resigned myself to the fact that I'm always going to be in recovery from something. But a dear friend reminded me that almost anyone who is breathing is likely in recovery. So yes, I'm in recovery from a handful of struggles and ailments—the latest being a depression that looks less like numbness and more like anger that has seeped into so many facets of my life.

"But some anger is good," I hear people say. "Anger can

give you the fuel you need to do the work, to bide the course, to keep the steam going and stay in the fight." Anger certainly does that for me, but I found that if it is all that's there, if anger alone is fueling the work each day, then something in me hardens, and the anger turns into cynicism, rather than something useful. Though the anger gave me energy when I was speaking into the darkness, something shifted when I felt swallowed up by it. I found I was tired. I don't mean just the "I haven't had normal sleep in over five years" kind of tired, nor the "My long run of the day is killing my feet, so I need new Brooks running shoes" kind of tired, nor the deadlines-coming-out-of-my ears kind of tired. And I mean more than the emotional and physical exhaustion of keeping up with the schedule of children, whether preschool or college aged.

Rather, in a feeling that persists today, I was tired of maintaining anger as if that were the only nourishment for this life. I was hungry—seriously, on my hands and knees famished—for something else. I longed for peace.

Peace has been chasing me down, especially these last couple of years, and lately it comes to me in snippets and morsels, like crumbs tossed off a table or scraps that have fallen off the kitchen counter. It arrives like flashes of light on my periphery as I grope my way through the darkness, trying to find a way out, and like the sound of a melody I once sang without even thinking about it but now can't remember. Thankfully, that peace is persistent; it won't give up on me, even if it shows up in the queerest ways.

Last year, a friend from high school painted me a modern

version of an icon of Saint Margaret. The painting was born from dreams and stories, conversations and revelations amalgamating various images. She came to me as I spent time working in specific spaces that provide not only hospitality but also solidarity with those displaced in our community, at low-barrier shelters and the local homeless community center.

Saint Margaret of Cortona is the patron saint of the disenfranchised and the marginalized. She began working with this population after losing the love of her life. A second Margaret—Saint Margaret of Scotland, queen of Scotland—was a Reformer, a subversive and influencer in her own right. She worked faithfully to enact numerous ecclesiastical reforms and to care for the orphans and poor. A bit more provocative but just as important to me is a third Margaret: Margaret Cho, a rare Asian American female comedian. I have grown to admire Cho's moxie in connecting art and politics. She is unabashedly who she is—something so refreshing in light of the culture of our childhood upbringing.

All these Margarets mark out a way through my own meandering in the wilderness. This queer icon, a beautiful rendition of Saint Margaret with an Asian face, kneeling in cutoff jeans, a basket of bread in one hand and a chalice in the other, tattoos of a labyrinth on one arm and the Chinese character for *journey* on the other, a dove hovering nearby—she is my pillar of cloud by day and fire by night. She is the possibility of a life lived radically, messily, and hopefully, in peace and in pursuit of peace, of peacemaking. She helps me imagine how to deliberately confront and co-opt anger—not letting it consume me, but not diminishing it or belittling it or trying to dress it up as something it is not. When tempered with the desire to surrender to peace, I can see anger produce the beginning glimmerings of a kind of wholeheartedness. I appreciate Brené Brown's take: "There are many tenets of Wholeheartedness, but at its very core is vulnerability and worthiness: facing uncertainty, exposure, and emotional risks, and knowing that I am enough."[4]

The pendulum swing between the struggle with anger and a longing for peace finds its equilibrium in knowing I am enough—that who I am is enough for the writing, the speaking and preaching, the parenting, the mentoring and ministering, the working that I do. Who I am is enough for these seasons, for this moment, for this living. I try too hard to do too many things awesomely, I realized one weekend when everything came to a head. I saw how much I lived frantically and frenetically in fear of scarcity, of not being enough, of failure, and I realized how that often fueled my anger.

Queerness is found in these spaces in between. For me, it is in the space between anger and peace. Healing makes space for all those emotions—the wide, varying spectrum, the multiplicities, complexities, the ineffable and inexpressible. The work of peacemaking means allowing for all of it, realizing it will never be easy or pretty, simple or straightforward, linear or formulaic.

My living into queerness is rooted in belovedness and the beloved community. A queer spirituality makes space for cultivating belovedness, and though I have struggled with obligations to the church (believing and thinking that my faith and spiritual practices had to happen in the church), without the local church I wouldn't have expanded my understanding of spirituality *and* church. The everyday practices of faith and spirituality meant I had to contend with depression and anger, but queerness was a way to understand how wholeheartedness makes space for all these experiences. It brought healing.

Yet, I'm still periodically paralyzed by feeling the crashing waves of anger or feeling hollow from the absence of peace. It is enough to derail any kind of exertion for work. In other words, I would rather stay in bed. Some days call for a return to the warmth of heavy quilts. But I will take a cue from my guide, Saint Margaret, to believe that peace isn't always accompanied by a feeling, but that it is a symptom of wholeheartedness. I will learn to trust the scars and markings of the journey on my life, to keep feeding and being fed by others, and to trust the presence of the Holy Spirit. I will keep on seeking and living that peace, because it will sustain my life. I will listen and wait, and let myself be astonished and nourished by the queer ways that peace, hope, joy, and most of all, love show up.

***

I write these words near the season of Advent, mindful of darkness and lighting candles, of waiting and anticipation, of moments pregnant with God's in-breaking, border-crossing self in Jesus the Christ. I have to temper the compulsion to break out all the festive lighting, red bows, and greens, the urge to make the leap to Christmas without proper time spent in the dusk of this season. It's hard to wait, particularly this year, when it feels we've been in a perpetual darkness at various levels—politically, globally, environmentally. And, we're in the midst of a daily onslaught of stories about the church's failures—the pain and hurt caused from the pulpit and the pews, the doors slammed shut in people's faces, the abuses that continue without atonement or redress within its hallowed walls.

A couple of years ago, I helped facilitate a Twitter conversation, "Why Church?" where participants wrestled with why we keep on with church. At its worst, the church is an instrument of exclusion, rejection, and even, yes, real violence. Sometimes the church at its best feels too polished and shiny, like the individual silver chalice cups my former church used during Communion. But the responses to "Why Church?" brought me to my knees. The tweets described healing and resurrection, discovering one's gifts, and finding a community who believes for you when you don't believe yourself. I remembered why I fell in love and what captured my soul about church, and now I think, "Yes, I'm staying. I'm not going anywhere." Because not only do I need church, the church needs me.

The church needs all of me. It needs all of my failures and flaws, all of my baggage, and even all of my struggles with ego and privilege, because that's where the transformation happens—in the midst of skin and bones, brutal vulnerability and weakness. It happens in the woods and in the delivery room, yes, but most certainly, it was meant to happen in community, in the sanctuary, in the light of the candles, around the font and the table. The church was given to us as a way to care for each other, a way to be a glimmering of heaven on earth and God's kingdom come. The church is meant to be food, meant to be breath, meant to be song, whether it's a meal made up of creamy soup and noodles or mashed-up food and crackers or gathering around a podcast sermon.

When asked, "Why church?" a queer spirituality says, "Because we believe in each other." That answer applies whatever the season or struggle, whatever the questions or conflict, whatever tables need to be overturned, and whatever rules need to be broken for the sake of salvation, whatever the level of belief or understanding, whatever the desire or doctrine. A queer spirituality sees the urgency of the time—that lives are on the brink, and what matters is our bodies. So a queer spirituality is capacious and abundant in its confessional and creedal expressions of love, of faith, of hope. When it comes to church, this means there's more than enough room around the table, in this pew, in the font, within the hallowed walls, and even in the pulpit for you, for me, for all of us.

We are called out, and we are called in. And we're called to be together. Being together matters. I matter. You matter. We matter together.

Notes

1. Penny Carothers, "The Desert Mothers Didn't Change Diapers, but Maybe They Should Have," *Storyline* (blog), October 26, 2011, https://tinyurl.com/y9qatapa.

2. John Steinbeck, *East of Eden* (New York: Penguin, 2002), 19.

3. Gloria Anzaldua, *Borderlands/La Frontera: The New Mestiza* (San Francisco: Aunt Lute, 1987), 25.

4. Brene Brown, *Daring Greatly: How the Courage to Be Vulnerable Transforms the Way We Live, Love, Parent, and Lead* (New York: Penguin, 2012), 29.

Afterword: Making Love as a Queer Spirituality

> I urge you all today, especially today during these times of chaos and war, to love yourself without reservations and to love each other without restraint. Unless you're into leather.
>
> —Margaret Cho, actress, comedian, icon

On June 12, 2016, Omar Mateen, a twenty-nine-year-old security guard, killed forty-nine people and wounded fifty-eight others in a terrorist attack and hate crime inside Pulse, a gay nightclub in Orlando, Florida. Later that day, I spent time in quiet with the queer icon of Saint Margaret, surrounded by candles, and meditated on these words by Margaret Cho. After thinking about leather and laughing through a few tears, I pondered what it means that making peace, hope, joy, and love are forms of resistance.

I have found a way to survive each day, each minute, by immersing myself in the writing and artistry of people of color, especially queer people of color: James Baldwin, Audre Lorde, José Esteban Muñoz, Andrew Ahn, Sara Ahmed,

207

Gloria Anzaldua. The literature and poetry, art and music, blogs and tweets of those who are right in the midst of struggle, loss, grief, and despair, flailing and barely keeping a head above water, are where I find the most resonance with my own life. No doubt, anyone would look at my life and see only too many reasons to be thankful, and most days, weeks, and months, I am. But we're social beings living in a globalized world, and we're moving through time and history unable to avoid so many intersecting realities, the clash between ideals and reality, and the subsequent fragmentation. Furthermore, individual persons hold within themselves whole universes—full of worlds of sorrow and desire. In other words, life is much more complicated beneath the surface.

So we have to do what we must to get through it all. As Gloria Anzaldua says, "Nobody's going to save you. No one's going to cut you down, cut the thorns thick around you. No one's going to storm the castle walls nor kiss awake your birth, climb down your hair, nor mount you onto the white steed. There is no one who will feed the yearning. Face it. You will have to do, do it yourself."[1] That is why we make ways to survive these days. We find strategies and mechanisms, and sometimes they involve bourbon or a good book or sex or a pint of ice cream. So much of queer spirituality is about resistance, and at the heart, this resistance is lovemaking. Or in Margaret Cho's words, it's loving oneself and loving each other.

It's love, and it's passion. A queer spirituality blurs the lines between both and recognizes the ways they are intertwined in our lives, even in scandalous ways, as in the opening poem called "Kissing God," to a chapter in *Indecent Theology*, which asks: What do you suppose it would be like to kiss God? Would it be a rush like sticking your tongue into a wall socket? Would you survive the experience? Would it be worth it?[2]

Christian history is full of stories of love and passion for God. The martyrs faced death to remain faithful. Activists and theologians who advocated for the poor gave their lives over to prisons and torture chambers. They could only do these things if their whole selves were completely overtaken with mad passion for their God of justice. These lovers of God would stick their tongues into a wall socket, and whether or not they survived, the experience would be worth it.

This kind of passion, sometimes expressed by illicit lovers who risk that embrace, is what fuels love and action, where "desire carries that life."[3] Desire coaxes and draws out, leads and pushes, pulls and compels us to live and love out loud. The cliché slogan Make Love, Not War makes sense. There is something profoundly revolutionary about lovemaking as a way to reject making death. It's resisting the darkness and destruction of life, of light and love. And while it's protesting, resisting, and surviving, it's also creating and making life in response to forces that would take away life. It's more than surviving; it's creating, thriving, and flourishing.

What I realize I need and want to be a part of is a kind of work that cultivates the expansiveness of love. I dream often of the kind of world we could have for us, for our children, if we weren't so concerned with regulating, disciplining, and closeting love all the time. If anything, it's absolutely clear that this world needs more love. Rather than focusing so much energy on categorizing and classifying sexuality and making it conform to narrow representations, I long for our world to encourage lovemaking, to spark in those around me a desire to love ourselves and love each other into more life and love. Because if there is anything I've learned about love, whether experienced among family, friends, or my children, it is that it is contagious and expands exponentially. It overflows the cup. Once released and liberated, it changes everything.

For me, ultimately, it's all about love. A dear friend, Jodi Houge, pastor of Humblewalk Church, a fiesty congregation in the Evangelical Lutheran Church of America, shared some thoughts with me from her sermon on the parable of the ten bridesmaids. In the parable, Jesus offers a picture of the kingdom of heaven by telling a story about ten bridesmaids who went to meet their bridegroom in the evening. Half of them forgot oil for their lamps, while the other half wisely took extra, so the second group entered the wedding banquet while the others were locked out when they went to buy more oil. It's a story that would dishearten, except that Jodi said, "These bridesmaids were foolish only in forgetting who the Bridegroom is. Love appears, with enough light for everyone. And if they miss Love this time around, there is another wedding next week, because this Bridegroom just keeps coming and coming and coming with light and love for you."

Love keeps coming and coming and coming. Love and light—this is what our lives need these days, and by God's grace, it's what I've experienced especially these recent few years, not only from the day I had children, or from the day I got married, but at significant points throughout my life that felt like huge ruptures in my world. It was love, always love bursting through what seemed like a hardened winter soil. Queerness took root, and it was the love of my community, the pursuit of a desiring God, the love of a queer Jesus, and the presence of the Holy Spirit that gave space for it to grow in the warmth of both sun and storm.

A queer spirituality transgresses the boundaries of how we live, move, and breathe through this world. It is truly embodied, and rooted in flesh-and-blood bodies, bodies that are surprising and show up as icons and words. It is also rooted in the body of Christ, in God-with-Us, in the continuous blurring of transcendence and immanence. That blurring feels like the essence of lovemaking, making love; any kind of crossing over is an intimacy, a mixing and mingling. It is also simultaneously rooted in the body of Christ, for queerness can't happen apart from the body.

When we embrace queerness, we make meaning through our bodies and with other bodies. We see, we speak, we work, we love, we discern, we prophesy, we dream, and we make meaning. And we do so in community, necessarily entangled and intertwined with each other.

I offer this short prayer written by another dear friend,
Emily Scott, for National Coming Out Day this past year,
because it fundamentally and thoroughly expresses what I feel
in my bones, and that is gratitude.

> For the ways, visible and invisible, that I am in-between,
> For movement toward an honest self that crashes through false
> binaries,
> For the freedoms, won by those before us and those among us
> and those who will come,
> to live in liminal ways,
> For Queering. For Queerness. I give thanks.

Notes

1. Gloria Anzaldúa and AnaLouise Keating, *The Gloria Anzaldúa Reader* (Durham: Duke University Press, 2009), 41.

2. Marcella Althaus-Reid, *Indecent Theology: Theological Perversions in Sex, Gender and Politics* (London: Routledge, 2000), 125.

3. Marcella Althaus-Reid, *Indecent Theology* (London: Routledge, 2002), 125.